CREATING 'CHURCH' AT HOME

For people living with anxiety or depression

Patrick Coghlan

kevin
mayhew

kevin mayhew

First published in Great Britain in 2016 by Kevin Mayhew Ltd
Buxhall, Stowmarket, Suffolk IP14 3BW
Tel: +44 (0) 1449 737978 Fax: +44 (0) 1449 737834
E-mail: info@kevinmayhew.com

www.kevinmayhew.com

9 8 7 6 5 4 3 2 1 0

ISBN 978 1 84867 841 5
Catalogue No. 1501518

Cover design by Rob Mortonson
© Image used under licence from Shutterstock Inc.
Edited by Nicki Copeland
Typeset by Angela Selfe
Proofread by Virginia Rounding

Printed and bound in Great Britain

Contents

WORSHIP SESSIONS

About the author

Patrick is Minister at Worstead Baptist Church in Meeting Hill (North Norfolk). He is a trustee and chaplain of Aylsham and district Care Trust (ACT), and manager of 4C's Aylsham Counselling Centre. ACT is a Christian community care charity, which is part of the St Michael's Care Complex in Aylsham, and the organisation does a lot of work with older people.

In his work as a minister, chaplain and counsellor, Patrick has had considerable experience of working with people of most age groups, in the context of providing ministry and care – many of whom have been quite vulnerable – including those living with varying types and degrees of dementia.

Patrick is married to June and they have two grown-up children – Rachel and Jonathan. For his leisure Patrick enjoys quality family time, walking the two family dogs and riding his red motorcycle.

Patrick has been an enthusiastic author for many years, having had his first book published in 2001. He has written a variety of Christian resources for different age groups, and some family novels.

Introduction

After being involved in a church fellowship – experiencing the spiritual input, support, encouragement, love and friendships it offers – a huge void must be left in people's lives when that is no longer possible, as a result of difficult or changing circumstances. I have written *Creating 'church' at home* with that in mind. My intention was to produce some ideas and material to enable an act of worship to take place in the home – even for those with no ministerial or leadership experience – and for it to be done in such a way that it would be deep and meaningful.

Creating 'church' at home is focused towards those who are housebound because of anxiety or depression and as a result are no longer able to get out to church activities or Bible studies. *Creating 'church' at home* can be used as a personal resource or may be enjoyed with one or two carers, friends, neighbours or family members. It is a user-friendly, off-the-page, Bible-based resource that has the flexibility of being adapted to different situations. More about that in the following chapters.

The approach taken by *Creating 'church' at home* is to build up an understanding of the individual who is housebound, – which may be yourself – as that will form the basis of the approach to the act of worship. This includes the style of the time of spiritual preparation leading into the act of worship and the way the room is set up for the occasion (in a way that is familiar, comfortable and meaningful).

There are three different contexts in which to use *Creating 'church' at home* (by using the different options in the worship sessions). These are described in detail in the following three chapters.

Housebound
Housebound with a friend
Carer for someone who is housebound

N.B. Using the short messages from the author (see 'How to use this book'), pick out which of these three chapters best describes your situation. Turn to the appropriate page: you only need to read that one chapter before beginning your preparations for the 25 ministry sessions that follow.

How to use this book

Using the short messages from the author (below), pick out which of the following best describes your situation. You only need to read that one chapter before beginning your preparations for the 25 ministry sessions that follow.

- You have become housebound as a result of anxiety or depression and, because you are not feeling ready to mix with others, are no longer able to regularly participate in the activities of your local church. If this describes your situation, and you want to enjoy a fulfilling act of worship at home, then chapter 1 is for you.

- You have become housebound as a result of anxiety or depression and, because you are not feeling ready to mix with others, are no longer able to regularly participate in the activities of your local church. However, you have a trusted friend, neighbour or family member who is happy to come in and join with you for a time of worship at home. If this describes your situation, then chapter 2 is for you.

- You are caring for someone (or are a good friend, neighbour or family member of someone) who has become housebound as a result of anxiety or depression. They are no longer able to regularly participate in the activities of their local church, and you want to organise worship sessions for them at home. If this describes your situation, chapter 3 is for you.

CHAPTER ONE

Housebound

You have become housebound as a result of anxiety or depression and, because you are not feeling ready to mix with others, are no longer able to regularly participate in the activities of your local church. If this describes your situation, and you want to enjoy a fulfilling act of worship at home, then this chapter is for you.

Getting to know you

As well as coming to terms with many other consequences of becoming housebound, if your faith and involvement in church activities has been a large part of your life (maybe for many years), you are probably struggling at times to find sufficient spiritual nourishment. But perhaps more than that, you could be finding it difficult to fully enter into worshipping God on your own. Maybe you dream that 'church' could be brought into your home.

We know that the Church is the people and not the building or its furnishings; however, it could be helpful to you to reproduce some of those elements that have been a part of your worship over the years – in your own home: those things that are familiar, comforting and helpful to your worship; things that will assist in making your worship personal; and things that will help you to connect with God and have a truly fulfilling worship experience.

The intention of *Creating 'church' at home* is to help you to replicate at least something of the church experience that you have been used to and have treasured – in order to help you to achieve a satisfying spiritual life.

Consider carefully your church background and preferences. Think about the following questions. The conclusions you arrive at will form the basis of how you could set the scene for your personal worship sessions (using the resources provided in *Creating 'church' at home*).

- What denomination have you been used to?

- Do you like a formal or an informal approach to worship?

- Is your preference for a modern or a more traditional style?

- How was the building in which you used to worship laid out?

- What are your favourite hymns, and what is your preferred style of church music?

- What is your preferred version of the Bible?

- Did you have a particular role in the church: for example, musician, choir member or worship leader, lay reader or local preacher, Sunday school teacher, flower arranger, etc.?

Setting the scene

Spend some time yourself – or ask a friend, neighbour or family member to help – collecting together some resources which will help to replicate something of the style and feeling of the place and situation where you have been used to worshipping in the past.

- Take your Bible readings from the version of the Bible that you prefer.

- If you have been used to having symbols like a cross, some candles or a banner to focus on at the front, get a small, free-standing cross, some candles (battery ones are probably safer in the home), a banner, etc. to re-create the feel of what you have been used to.

- You might like to brighten up the room with some flowers or a flowering plant, placed somewhere prominent.

- You may already have some CDs of the kind of church music that you like and feel comfortable with: have one playing quietly in the background to lead into your worship session.

- If you were a church musician and you have an instrument at home, you might like to provide the music yourself.

- If you were in the choir, a worship leader or an enthusiastic singer, you might like to join in and sing with the CD.

- If you were involved in a teaching ministry, I am sure you can add your mark to the sessions in some way.

- This is your time and setting: do with it exactly as you would like.

Guide to using the material

- Set out the room – including the music playing quietly in the background.

- **Be still and quiet:** Spend some time being still and quiet in God's presence, listening to the background music which is playing, in preparation for using the resources provided for your act of personal worship. Focus on the theme during this time.

- **Passage to read:** The Bible references for a psalm or part of a psalm to read. Read it out loud if you prefer.

- Select **(Option 1) Resting in his presence:** Listening to, and receiving restoration, guidance and healing from

God. This is linked with or in some way leads into the main theme of the session.

- **Story to tell (in the author's words):** Read this familiar Bible story (out loud if you prefer), which is told in the author's own words (Bible references are given). The author endeavours to bring out a spiritual message at the end of the retelling of the story, as indicated by the subheading.

- **Prayer of response and the Lord's Prayer:** Draw the session to a positive close. (The bracketed words are either allowing for additional material or, in most cases, for use in a shared worship session.)

- **Be still and quiet:** If you would like to, spend some further time in God's presence in an attitude of worship as you listen to the CD again (or sing or play some more music yourself).

CHAPTER TWO

Housebound with a friend

You have become housebound as a result of anxiety or depression and, because you are not feeling ready to mix with others, are no longer able to regularly participate in the activities of your local church. However, you have a trusted friend, neighbour or family member who is happy to come in and join with you for a time of worship at home. If this describes your situation, then this chapter is for you.

Getting to know you both

As well as coming to terms with many other consequences of becoming housebound, if your faith and involvement in church activities has been a large part of your life (maybe for many years), you are probably struggling at times to find sufficient spiritual nourishment. But perhaps more than that, you could be finding it difficult to fully enter into worshipping God on your own. Maybe you dream that 'church' could be brought into your home. Now you have a friend, neighbour or family member who is happy to come and share with you to make that something of a reality.

We know that the Church is the people and not the building or its furnishings; however, it could be helpful to you to reproduce some of those elements that have been a part of your worship (and that of your friend, neighbour or family member) over the years – in your own home: those things that are familiar, comforting and helpful to your worship; things that will assist in making your worship personal; and things that will help you both to connect with God and have a truly fulfilling worship experience.

The intention of Creating 'church' at home is to endeavour to help you to replicate at least something of the church experience that you have both been used to and have treasured – in order to help you to achieve a satisfying spiritual life.

Consider carefully your own church background and preferences and those of the person who is coming to share the worship sessions with you. Discuss together the following questions. The conclusions you arrive at will form the basis of how you could set the scene for your shared worship sessions (using the resources provided in Creating 'church' at home).

- What denominations have you both been used to?

- Do you both like a formal or an informal approach to worship? Or have you come from different church backgrounds with contrasting approaches?

- Are both your preferences for a modern or a more traditional style? Or do you have different preferences?

- How was the building in which you both used to worship laid out? Or did you worship in different churches with completely different layouts?

- What are your favourite hymns, and what is your preferred style of church music? Between you, there could be quite a wide range of choices.

- What is your preferred version of the Bible? You might not both make the same choice.

- Did either of you have a particular role in the church: for example, musician, choir member or worship leader, lay reader or local preacher, Sunday school teacher, flower arranger, etc.?

Setting the scene

Spend some time with your friend, neighbour or family member collecting together some resources which will help to replicate something of the style and feeling of the places and situations where you have both been used to worshipping in the past. You might not necessarily have the same views about everything, but I am sure you will be able to come to an agreement, which may involve taking turns or making a compromise.

- Take your Bible readings from the version of the Bible that you prefer.

- If you have been used to having symbols like a cross, some candles or a banner to focus on at the front, get a small, free-standing cross, some candles (battery ones are probably safer in the home), a banner, etc. to re-create the feel of what you have been used to.

- You might like to brighten up the room with some flowers or a flowering plant, placed somewhere prominent.

- You may already have some CDs of the kind of church music that you like and feel comfortable with: have one playing quietly in the background at the beginning of your worship session.

- If either of you were a church musician and you have an instrument, you might like to provide the music yourselves.

- If either of you were in the choir, a worship leader or an enthusiastic singer, you might like to join in and sing with the CD.

- If either of you were involved in teaching ministry, then I am sure you can add your marks to the sessions in some way.

- It is your time and setting: do with it exactly as you both would like.

Guide to using the material

- Set out the room – including the music playing quietly in the background.

- **Be still and quiet:** Spend some time being still and quiet in God's presence, listening to the background music which is playing, in preparation for using the resources provided for your act of shared worship. Focus on the theme during this time.

- **Passage to read:** The Bible references for a psalm or part of a psalm to read out loud.

- Select **(Option 2) Coffee time :** An opportunity to discuss feelings, fears and anxieties informally over a hot drink. This is linked with or in some way leads into the theme of this session. Make a confidentiality agreement between you both to provide the safety to share.

- **Story to tell (in the author's words):** Read this familiar Bible story out loud, which is told in the author's own words (Bible references are given). The author endeavours to bring out a spiritual message at the end of the retelling of the story, as indicated by the subheading.

- **Prayer of response and the Lord's Prayer:** Draw the session to a close in a positive way. (The bracketed words are either allowing for additional material or, in most cases, for use in a shared worship session.)

- **Be still and quiet:** If you would both like to, spend some more time in God's presence in a continued attitude of worship as you listen to the CD again (or sing or play some more music yourselves).

CHAPTER THREE

Carer for someone who is housebound

You are caring for someone (or are a good friend, neighbour or family member of someone) who has become housebound as a result of anxiety or depression. They are no longer able to regularly participate in the activities of their local church, and you want to organise worship sessions for them at home. If this describes your situation, then this chapter is for you.

Getting to know the person

People who are housebound still have spiritual needs. This is highlighted if they have a strong faith and have been actively involved in the church in the past (maybe for many years). Try to imagine the frustration of no longer being able to attend or fully engage in public worship, group Bible studies or having fellowship with Christians in other ways. You have picked up this resource on behalf of someone who is in that position, and you are hoping to draw alongside them in an endeavour to help them to find greater satisfaction in their spiritual life.

We know that the Church is the people and not the building or its furnishings; however, it could be helpful to that person who is housebound if you are able to reproduce some of those elements that have been part of their worship over the years – in their own home: those things that are familiar, comforting and helpful to their worship; things that will assist in making their worship personal; and things that will help them to connect with God and have a truly fulfilling worship experience.

The intention of *Creating 'church' at home* is to endeavour to help you to replicate at least something of the church experience that the recipient has been used to and has treasured – in order to help them to achieve a satisfying spiritual life.

You are a carer, friend, neighbour or family member of the recipient. I would encourage you to find out as much as you can about the church background and preferences of that person, in order to make their worship experience really count. Discuss the following questions with the recipient, and maybe (with their permission) chat to their minister. The conclusions you arrive at will form the basis of how you could set the scene for your shared worship sessions (using the worship material provided in *Creating 'church' at home*).

- What denomination has the recipient been used to?

- Does the recipient like a formal or an informal approach to worship?

- Is the recipient's preference for a modern or a more traditional style?

- How was the building in which the recipient's worship took place laid out?

- What are the recipient's favourite hymns, and what is their preferred style of music?

- What is the recipient's preferred version of the Bible?

- Did the recipient have a particular role in the church: for example, musician, choir member or worship leader, lay reader or local preacher, Sunday school teacher, flower arranger, etc?

Setting the scene

Spend some time collecting together some resources which will help you to replicate something of the style and feelings of the place and situation where the recipient has been used to worshipping in the past. The recipient themselves may like to help with this process.

- Take the Bible readings from the version of the Bible that the recipient prefers.

- If the recipient has been used to having symbols like a cross, some candles or a banner to focus on at the front, get a small, free-standing cross, some candles (battery ones are probably safer in the home), a banner, etc. to re-create the feel of what they have been used to.

- You might like to brighten up the room with some flowers or a flowering plant, placed somewhere prominent.

- The recipient may already have some CDs of the kind of church music that they like and feel comfortable with: have one playing quietly in the background at the beginning of the worship session.

- If the recipient was a church musician and has an instrument, they might like to provide the music themselves.

- If the recipient was in the choir, a worship leader or an enthusiastic singer, they might like to join in and sing with the CD.

- If the recipient was involved in a teaching ministry, I am sure that they can add their mark to the sessions in some way.

- It is the recipient's time and setting: do with it exactly as they would like.

Guide to using the material

- Set out the room – including the music playing quietly in the background.

- **Be still and quiet:** Spend some time sitting with the recipient. Be still and quiet in God's presence, listening to the background music which is playing, in preparation for using the resources provided in your act of shared worship. Try to both focus on the theme during this time.

- **Passage to read:** The Bible references for a psalm or part of a psalm to read out loud.

- Select **(Option 3) Make a plan:** Spend some time thinking and chatting about setting achievable goals, making necessary changes and building up hopes for the immediate future informally over a cup of tea or coffee. This is linked with or in some way leads into the theme of this session. It is a good idea to make some notes either in a notebook or electronically.

- **Story to tell (in the author's words):** Read this familiar Bible story out loud, which is told in the author's own words (Bible references are given). The author endeavours to bring out a spiritual message at the end of the retelling of the story, as indicated by the subheading.

- **Prayer of response and the Lord's Prayer:** Draw the session to a close in a positive way. (The bracketed words are either allowing for additional material or, in most cases, for use in a shared worship session.)

- **Be still and quiet:** If the recipient would like to, spend some more time in God's presence in an attitude of worship as you listen to the CD again (or sing or play some more music yourselves).

WORSHIP SESSIONS

PART ONE

The Church Calendar

Lent

Be still and quiet: Being prepared – Making a response to Jesus' death and resurrection.

Passage to read: Psalm 15.

(Option 1)
Resting in his presence: Pray the following short prayer and then spend a few minutes allowing Jesus to fill you with his love, comfort, peace and strength.

Lord Jesus, please help me to feel held by you, in a close relationship, during this difficult time in my life.
Amen.

(Option 2)
Coffee time: Chat over a hot drink about what kind of lifestyle might evidence a true commitment to following Jesus. At this time you might be struggling to feel close to Jesus: if you can, spend some time talking about how you are feeling right now.

(Option 3)
Make a plan (begin with the prayer – Lord, reveal your plan. Amen): Talk about where you might like to go for an outing when you are feeling better – it needs to be a realistic aim. What preparations would you need to make on the day?

Story to tell (in the author's words):
(Based on Matthew 25:1-13)

Jesus told this parable as a way of explaining what the kingdom of heaven would be like.

Ten young ladies had been invited to a wedding: five were wise and five were not so wise. They arrived for the celebrations – dressed up for the occasion – only to discover that the bridegroom still hadn't arrived. It was getting quite late – and dark – so it was a good job the ladies had brought their oil lamps with them.

There was a lot of laughter and chatter while they were sitting waiting, and the time passed quite quickly. Indeed, it got very late, and the groom had still not arrived. At that point, some of the lamps began to flicker – a sure sign that the oil was running low. Fortunately, the five wise ladies had brought some spare oil. They hurriedly topped up their lamps, and carried on chatting. However, the five not-so-wise ladies had not come prepared.

'Can you spare us some of your oil?' they pleaded to the wiser members of the party.

'No, we can't; because then we will run short. You should have thought about this when you got ready to come!'

After a few minutes' thought, the not-so-wise ladies jumped up. 'We're just popping out to see if we can buy some more oil. Wait for us if the groom arrives while we're away.'

And the bridegroom did arrive in their absence; but there wasn't time to wait.

'Come on in, ladies, and join the celebrations,' the groom invited.

The five wise ladies who were there – prepared, ready and waiting – hurried in, before the door was firmly shut and locked behind them. The wedding banquet was laid out: it looked amazing – so much lovely food and drink. Time to party!

When the not-so-wise ladies arrived back, having bought some more oil, they banged on the door. 'Open up and let us in! Sorry we're late!'

But they were not allowed in, because they had not been prepared and ready for the arrival of the bridegroom. What a tragic end to the story!

What it means to be spiritually prepared

Jesus is talking about his return (his second coming); he is pleading with us to be spiritually prepared for that time by making a positive response to his death and resurrection – entering into a personal relationship with him. The wedding feast represents the ultimate fulfilment of the kingdom. All the young ladies represent those who profess to be followers of Jesus. Those who come prepared with spare oil represent those whose commitment of faith is evidenced by an appropriate lifestyle. Those who come unprepared represent those whose profession of faith has no real evidence in their lifestyle. The message is that only those who are truly prepared will enter into God's eternal kingdom.

In times of sickness (mental or physical) we can find ourselves becoming more aware of our mortality, and as a result thinking more about what happens after death, and whether or not we are prepared for that time. This story becomes particularly relevant if that is where you are in your life's journey.

Prayer (renewing, affirming and strengthening our relationship and daily walk with Jesus):

Lord Jesus,
as I (we) think about being prepared for Easter and the significance of the events to me (us) today, I (we) also think about being prepared for your second coming.
Fill me (us) with a sense of urgency to be ready for your return. During this period of Lent, help me (us) to look seriously at my (our) relationship with you, and to think about how your death, resurrection and ascension are relevant to me (us) today. Let this be a time of Bible study, prayer and listening to your answers.
Help me (us) to walk closer to you day by day, and to evidence my (our) faith by living out an appropriate lifestyle – living according to your teaching and example.
I (We) pray for those who are not prepared for your return. Amen.

Finish with the Lord's Prayer.

Mothering Sunday

Be still and quiet: The parenthood of God – being part of God's family.

Passage to read: Psalm 68:4-6.

(Option 1)
Resting in his presence: Whatever your personal experience of a parent's love has been – good or bad – God is the perfect parent. Pray the following short prayer and then spend a few minutes allowing God to reveal something of his parenthood to you.

Loving heavenly Father, please help me to experience your perfect parenthood in my life. In Jesus' name.
Amen.

(Option 2)
Coffee time: Chat over a hot drink about parents and being a parent. What feelings do you associate with each?

(Option 3)
Make a plan (begin with the prayer – Lord, reveal your plan. Amen): Maybe since you have been feeling anxious or depressed you have struggled to keep in contact with family members – including those from the church family. Perhaps the plan could include setting times and dates to make some phone calls, send some emails, etc. to renew those contacts.

Story to tell (in the author's words):
(Based on Luke 15:11-32)

You probably know this story – it must be one of the most well known of Jesus' parables – but don't worry if you're not familiar with it.

It all started on a family farm in the countryside. A father and his two sons worked together growing crops and caring for livestock. The elder of the two sons was totally dedicated to his father and the farm, but the younger son was unsettled: he believed he was missing out on something. And so, one day he asked his father if they could have a chat.

The loving father smiled at his son. 'What is it?'

The younger son didn't believe in beating about the bush. 'I want my money now. I want my share of what the farm is worth so that I can go out and be free – live my life!'

His father could have refused, but he knew that his son would only become more restless and rebellious. 'Come and see me tomorrow, and I will give you the value of your inheritance.'

The next day, bags packed and a wallet stuffed full of money, the young man waved goodbye to his old life, and began his journey. He believed that this was true freedom and the route to unending joy. With so much money he could travel, party, have as many girlfriends as he liked and be thoroughly extravagant. Indeed, the women flocked to him, and he was surrounded by friends – he'd never been so popular before. But what he didn't realise was how quickly the money was going. Before very long he was broke. And he got caught up in a severe famine.

'Lend some money to your old friend, just to tide me over,' he asked his so-called best mate.

'You've got to be joking. You're no friend of mine!'

A day or two later the young runaway managed to get a job on a pig farm. It was hard work, and the pay was rubbish. He felt so hungry as he thought about how well fed he had always been at home. And he missed his dad so much – and even his older brother (though they hadn't always seen eye to eye).

'I can't go home, not after letting Dad down so badly,' he told himself for several weeks – until eventually he became so desperate that he decided he would return.

It was a long way. But what the lad didn't realise was that every day since he had left home, his father had walked out to the open plains to see if he could see his lost son returning in the distance. So while the young man was rehearsing what he would say to his dad, he was spotted in the distance. Despite the heat of the day, the boy's father ran for all he was worth to meet his returning son.

'Accept me back as one of your servants, if you will . . . please,' the boy mumbled.

'Come here and give your old dad a big hug, and stop all that nonsense about being a servant,' his father said as he flung his arms around his son.

There was a big party that evening, and although the lad's older brother was a bit put out – to say the least – his father explained that he loved them both equally.

Belonging to God's family

What an amazing father! So loving, generous, welcoming, forgiving and faithful. The younger son doesn't really deserve his father's kindness. And the older son is a little self-centred about his brother's return – although maybe understandably so.

This is a story about God's amazing love for each one of us. The younger son is like us when we turn our backs on God, tempted to satisfy our self-centred desires. The older son is like us when maybe we are a little self-righteous and judgemental. But the thing that really stands out is the amazing forgiveness that the father offers – the same forgiveness that God offers to us today!

God longs for us to be part of his heavenly family, and to experience his parenthood forever. In sickness (physical and mental), often family takes on a far greater significance than ever before. How significant is God's family in your life?

Prayer (giving thanks for mums, asking a blessing on parents and families, and giving thanks for and asking to be included in God's heavenly family):

Heavenly Father,
thank you that whatever I (we) do, you never stop loving me (us).
Thank you that even if I (we) have turned my (our) back(s) on you to go my (our) own way, you receive me (us) back with a warm welcome and forgiveness.
Help me (us) to be willing to be part of your family.
Thank you for earthly parents – especially mums!
Be with me as a (all of us who are) parent(s), grandparent(s) or great-grandparent(s) and help me (us) in the role(s) that I (we) play.

Fill me (us) with your love to share – and give me (us) wisdom. Thank you for my family (our families) which is (are) so important to me (us).
I (We) pray for a blessing upon all families.
In Jesus' name.
Amen.

Finish with the Lord's Prayer.

Palm Sunday

Be still and quiet: Jesus' victorious return – the victory has been won over sin and evil; share the joy and celebration.

Passage to read: Psalm 98.

(Option 1)
Resting in his presence: Spend a few minutes recalling some of the positive memories surrounding an occasion when a friend or family member returned after a long absence. Imagine what it will be like when Jesus returns.

(Option 2)
Coffee time: Chat over a hot drink about a surprise visit – when a visitor arrived completely unexpectedly. Talk about your feelings – did they change during the course of the visit? How do you feel about Jesus' promised return?

(Option 3)
Make a plan (begin with the prayer – Lord, reveal your plan. Amen)**:** Is there a close friend or family member who you haven't seen for a while who you would particularly like to spend some time with? Could this be something to put on the calendar to arrange in the not-too-distant future?

Story to tell (in the author's words):
(Based on Luke 19:28-48)

This story has to be one of the most visual stories in the New Testament, and it is a very important story for a number of reasons – so here goes!

Jesus was fast approaching the villages of Bethphage and Bethany when he called two of his disciples over for a word. 'I have a job for you two. I want you to go ahead of us into the village to get a donkey, please.'

There were some blank looks. 'What?'

Jesus elaborated. 'When you reach the village you will see a donkey colt tied up. I want you to untie it and bring it back here to me.'

'What if someone says something to us? What should we say?'

Jesus smiled convincingly. 'Just tell them that I need it.'

It happened just as Jesus had said it would. The two disciples found the colt. The owner spotted them and asked what they thought they were doing. They gave the reply, 'The Lord needs him.' And the owner was happy with that.

'But what's it for?' The disciples asked when the two arrived back.

Jesus turned to them, smiling. 'I'm going to ride him, of course.'

So the disciples threw a couple of cloaks across the animal's back and held onto the beast while Jesus got on. 'Where are you going?'

'We are going to continue on into Jerusalem.'

As Jesus approached Jerusalem on the back of the donkey, a crowd built up and people began to spread their cloaks out on the road in front. In loud voices they shouted praises to Jesus for all the miracles they had seen him perform. In a humble way, it reflected the return of a victorious king. It was indeed a joyous occasion, but there was a sadness in Jesus' heart as he rode towards his destination. He knew that his triumphal entry would spark a great deal of resistance to him and his ministry, and would eventually lead to his death on a cross.

Once in Jerusalem, Jesus entered into the temple – as he had before. But he was horrified to see all the traders busy doing business in the temple on this occasion.

'This is supposed to be a place of prayer,' he said in a very loud voice, 'and look what you have turned it into.' With that, Jesus began to drive them out.

Every day, Jesus went into the temple, teaching those who came to listen to him. He was a very popular figure with many people, although there were those who stood in the background watching and plotting his death. But it was difficult for them to do anything when Jesus was always surrounded by crowds of people who were hanging on to every word that he said. And so those who were against Jesus (like the chief priests and teachers of the law) were biding their time very carefully.

Celebrate Jesus' victory and experience the joy

There are various things going on during what we know as Palm Sunday:

The event is confrontational to those who oppose Jesus, especially when he goes into the temple and begins to drive the traders out. There are those who begin to plot against him. So by entering into Jerusalem, Jesus understands that he is heading towards his death on the cross; but he shows his willingness to still be part of the Father's plan.

Also, importantly, it is symbolic of the triumphal entry of a king victoriously returning from the battlefield, to rule his kingdom. This predicts Jesus' second coming, victorious over sin, evil and death, when his kingdom will reach its ultimate fulfilment. For those who are followers of Jesus it will be a time of joy and celebration as we share in the victory (see Revelation 17:14)!

At the present time, maybe you are not really feeling like partying. However, try not to let it compromise your anticipation of the celebration and eternal joy we will experience when Jesus returns, when, as followers of him, we will experience the kingdom in all its fullness.

Prayer (giving thanks for the promise that we as followers of Jesus will share in Jesus' victory over sin and evil, when he returns):

Lord Jesus,
thank you that though we are still in the spiritual battle, you have won the ultimate victory over sin and evil, through your death and resurrection.
Thank you that, as a result of the victory, when you return, your kingdom will reach its ultimate fulfilment, and you will rule as King.

Thank you that as a follower (as followers) of you, I (we) will share in that victory – and be part of your eternal kingdom. Thank you that everyone has the opportunity to be there! Encourage people to choose to follow you.

Thank you for the joy and sense of celebration that is promised when you return, which nothing can take away from us. Amen.

Finish with the Lord's Prayer.

Maundy Thursday

Be still and quiet: 'God willing' – accepting and doing God's will.

Passage to read: Psalm 40:1-8.

(Option 1)
Resting in his presence: Spend some time meditating on the thought that God is in control and he can bring something good even from the most difficult situation (Romans 8:28).

(Option 2)
Coffee time: Chat over a hot drink about those times when it is difficult to do God's will – and why? How does that make you feel?

(Option 3)
Make a plan (begin with the prayer – Lord, reveal your plan. Amen)**:** Decide on a 'to do' list for the day ahead, and talk about what it means to say, 'God willing'.

Story to tell (in the author's words):
(Based on Matthew 26:36-46)

> Jesus and his disciples were walking towards Gethsemane. There wasn't a great deal of conversation on the way after the things that had been said by Jesus earlier in the day about his death. The mood was sombre on their arrival.

Jesus turned to his disciples. 'Sit down on the grass and wait for me while I go and pray.' He was experiencing deep emotions as he took Peter, James and John further on with him. 'Keep alert while I go and pray.'

Jesus pleaded with the Father that he might be set free from the suffering and painful death that lay before him. He finished his prayer with the words, 'But it's not what I want; it is your will that should be done.'

Returning to his disciples, Jesus was disappointed that they had fallen asleep. Once again he asked them to remain alert, and this time also to join him in praying, commenting, 'I know that you have good intentions, but the body is weak.'

Jesus went away again to pray. This time he prayed that if a painful death on the cross were the only way, then so be it – finishing with the words, 'It is your will that should be done.'

On his return to the disciples Jesus found them sleeping again, so he left them, returning to pray for a third time. Once again Jesus finished his prayer with, 'It is your will that should be done.'

As Jesus walked back to where his disciples were sleeping, he had his answer from the Father: he knew exactly what he should do. 'Wake up. It's time. My betrayer is approaching.'

God's will be done

It is easy for us to fall into the trap of believing that, as Jesus approaches a terrible death on the cross, he is quite at ease about it. But that is not the case: the humanity of Jesus means that he feels the pain and the emotions that we feel – but his priority is always to do the Father's will.

There are life experiences that we struggle with. We shouldn't feel guilty if we battle with our feelings linked to those events. But we should always strive to accept the Father's will in all situations.

As we get older, and time seems to go so much faster, we might reach the point of becoming more aware of the value of each day – a gift from God. And so the saying 'God willing' begins to have far greater significance to us. However, if we are feeling stressed or our mood is low, as a result of anxiety or depression, it can be quite difficult to begin the day with a positive attitude; but it can be a tremendous comfort to know that God has his hand on us and is in control.

Prayer (for the strength to live according to God's will):

Loving heavenly Father,
thank you for the gift of time. Help me (us) to value it even when it seems difficult to do so, and grant me (us) the enablement to fit into the day those things that are important.
Thank you that your will is perfect.
Be with me (us) during those difficult and testing circumstances that I (we) will meet during my (our) life's journey: strengthen and uphold me (us).
But help me (us) to always accept and live according to your will.
I (We) pray that your will be done on earth.
In Jesus' name.
Amen.

Finish with the Lord's Prayer.

Good Friday

Be still and quiet: Jesus' death on the cross – the penalty for sin has been paid in full.

Passage to read: Psalm 67.

(Option 1)
Resting in his presence: Close your eyes for a few minutes and visualise 'freedom' as a seagull in flight: gracefully and repeatedly soaring up into the sky and then diving.

(Option 2)
Coffee time: Chat over a hot drink about what sin is, and in what capacity we have all sinned (see Romans 3:23). What would (does) it feel like to be set free from the consequences of sin – including feelings of guilt and remorse?

(Option 3)
Make a plan (begin with the prayer – Lord, reveal your plan. Amen)**:** Choose one of the Ten Commandments (Exodus 20:1-17), either the one that you feel is most applicable to you or one that you struggle to obey. Make it an aim to apply it to your lifestyle choices.

Story to tell (in the author's words):
(Based on Luke 23:26-49)

> It was a long, sad procession that headed towards Calvary. A man called Simon had been forced to carry the cross that Jesus was to be crucified on.

Perhaps the Romans feared that, if he were made to carry the heavy cross, Jesus might die before they reached their destination. And there were two other men, both criminals, who were led out to be crucified with Jesus. One was put to death on each side of Jesus.

We cannot even begin to imagine the pain and suffering that Jesus went through on the cross that day. The rustic nails that were driven through his hands and feet were probably hardly sharp enough to penetrate. Then there was the heat of the day, the pain, the trauma, and the ridicule . . . Every breath of air a struggle.

Apparently, onlookers divided up his clothes between them.

But Jesus looked down lovingly at those who were responsible for his death. 'Forgive them, Father.'

Soldiers offered Jesus wine vinegar and jeered at him: 'Get yourself down from there, you so-called King of the Jews!' Someone had attached a notice to the cross above Jesus' head, to that effect.

And then one of the criminals started to join in with the ridicule, 'If you really are the Messiah, you could save all three of us.'

The other criminal jumped to Jesus' defence. 'We deserve this; we are paying the penalty for our crimes, but this man has done nothing wrong.' Then he turned to Jesus. 'Remember me when you come into your kingdom.'

Jesus smiled. 'Of course. You will be with me in paradise today.'

Soon after that, Jesus cried out to the Father and died.

The price has been paid

There are three things that really stand out in this story. The first is the depth of love Jesus has for each one of us – that he is prepared to suffer and die in such a terrible way to pay the penalty for our sin. The second is the amazing faith of the criminal who asks Jesus to remember him. And the third is the instant forgiveness of that criminal and his eternal reward.

Jesus has paid the price that no one else could pay! He has made it possible for us to be forgiven and to live in his presence for eternity – surrounded by his blessing.

There is a tendency as we get older to look back over the years – maybe with some regrets. Most of us are prepared to admit that sometimes we have 'got it wrong': we have made bad decisions, we have not always been entirely honest, sometimes we have been selfish, at times we have responded in thoughtless ways, and so on. Guilt and low self-esteem can weigh heavily; especially when we are living with anxiety or depression. But the message of Good Friday is not about feeling a failure or being a bad person; it's about reaching out for forgiveness – forgiveness so complete that our sin is as far away from us as the East is from the West (see Psalm103:12).

Prayer (giving thanks that the penalty for sin has been paid, through Jesus' act of love on the cross):

Lord Jesus,

thank you for your amazing love for everyone, and that you died on the cross, paying the price that no one else could afford – paying the penalty for sin.

Thank you that by so doing, you have made it possible for everyone to be forgiven, and to be assured of an eternal place in your heavenly kingdom.

Help me (us) to recognise that I am (we are all) guilty of sin, as I (we) approach you in repentance and faith.
Forgive me (us) for those times that I (we) have 'got it wrong'.
Let others hear and respond to the message that the price for sin has been paid!
In your name.
Amen.

Finish with the Lord's Prayer.

Easter Sunday

Be still and quiet: Life after death – heaven.

Passage to read: Psalm 23.

(Option 1)
Resting in his presence: Heaven is about being in the Triune God's (God the Father, Jesus the Son and the Holy Spirit) presence forever – but without anything bad or negative to spoil it. Pray the following short prayer and then spend some quality time with God.

Loving God, please help me to spend some time resting in your presence today. In Jesus' name.
Amen.

(Option 2)
Coffee time: Chat over a hot drink about the springtime, and the new shoots springing up from what appear to be lifeless plants. This concept is used to represent Easter Sunday as a day of celebration in the Christian Church – Jesus coming to life again. But maybe you are not really feeling like celebrating today. Talk about how you are feeling right now.

(Option 3)
Make a plan (begin with the prayer – Lord, reveal your plan. Amen): Spring is here! Plan one or two achievable gardening jobs to perform over the next few days. Think particularly about clearing up the flower beds to allow the spring flowers the space to shoot and grow once more.

Story to tell (in the author's words):
(Based on Luke 24:13-35)

Their hearts were very heavy as Cleopas and his friend were walking from Jerusalem to Emmaus. The journey was about seven miles – but it seemed further! They were speaking about the traumatic events of the past few days, when suddenly a stranger joined them and began to walk with them.

The stranger enquired, 'What are you talking about?'

The two travellers came to a halt, turning to him in surprise. One of them questioned, 'Haven't you heard about the things that have happened?'

'What things?'

The traveller explained, 'Jesus of Nazareth has been crucified. We had hoped that he was the Messiah – what a disappointment! But then some of the women went to the tomb this morning and had a vision of angels who told them that Jesus was alive. Some of the others went to the tomb later in the day, and they confirmed what the women had said. Now we don't know what to think or believe.'

The stranger looked saddened. 'But the prophets said that the Messiah would suffer.' He went on to explain the meaning of the Scriptures concerning the Messiah as the others listened carefully.

When they arrived at Emmaus, the stranger acted as if he were going to continue on his journey. The others urged, 'It's late! Will you not stay with us tonight?'

The stranger smiled warmly. 'I appreciate that, thank you.'

During dinner, the stranger picked up a fresh loaf of bread, gave thanks to God and broke it, handing it round to everyone at the table. It was one of those moments of realisation, but at that instant in time the stranger disappeared.

'Why didn't we recognise that it was Jesus?' one of the travellers questioned in complete disbelief. 'It was so obvious!'

'There was something so special about the way he explained the Scriptures: we should have known,' the other added.

But, of course, they had been prevented from recognising Jesus until the moment he broke the bread, in the way he had done so many times before.

The two men couldn't contain their excitement. 'We have to go back to Jerusalem, right now, and tell the others that Jesus really has risen from the dead.'

A home in heaven

So what is the message of Easter Sunday? It's quite simple really: Jesus rose from the dead and is alive today. Death is not the end when we have a personal relationship with him. There is life after death, which the daffodils – associated with the springtime and Easter – have come to symbolise! And there is a heaven!

The older we get, perhaps the more significant the hope of heaven becomes – especially in times of bereavement, when we become more aware of our own mortality and seek some kind of comfort for that person who has passed away. (I appreciate, of course, that it is not just older people who meet with bereavement.)

Prayer (giving thanks for, and finding hope in the promise of eternal life):

Loving heavenly Father,
thank you that Jesus rose from the dead and is alive today.
Thank you that he has conquered death.
Thank you that through my (our) relationship with Jesus,
I am (we are) assured of life after death – in heaven.
Help me (us) to hold on to that hope.
I (We) pray that others might think seriously about their eternal future.
In Jesus' name.
Amen.

Finish with the Lord's Prayer.

Ascension

Be still and quiet: Jesus will return – completing the plan and a new beginning.

Passage to read: Psalm 27.

(Option 1)
Resting in his presence: A friend of mine who is a farmer spoke once about the promise of a fresh start when a field has been freshly ploughed. Close your eyes and visualise a field that is being ploughed. The birds follow the tractor and plough expectantly. Half the field is a mixture of stubble and weeds, the other half is fresh dark soil. Think about new beginnings.

(Option 2)
Coffee time: Chat over a hot drink about how you would feel if Jesus were to return unexpectedly tomorrow.

(Option 3)
Make a plan (begin with the prayer – Lord, reveal your plan. Amen): Plan some small jobs to do around the house: for example, washing up, tidying the breakfast things, putting clean washing in the drawers, cleaning shoes. When the job is finished, feel the satisfaction associated with starting and finishing a job – big or small.

Story to tell (in the author's words):
(Based on Acts 1:1-11)

Let me put a question to you: Why did Jesus make so many resurrection appearances to so many different people? Maybe you have an answer, or perhaps it's something you have never considered.

After Jesus rose from the dead, God's plan was that there would be indisputable proof that Jesus was alive; namely, that lots of people would witness the risen Jesus. And they did!

Following his resurrection but while he was still on earth, Jesus instructed his apostles, 'Stay in Jerusalem until you receive the power of the indwelling Holy Spirit. He will equip you to be my witnesses all over the world.'

Then Jesus ascended into heaven right in front of them. They watched until a cloud obscured their vision. The group of onlookers were still gazing up into the sky when they realised they had company. Two angelic beings were standing beside them – dressed in white.

'What are you looking at?' they quizzed. The group were speechless. 'Jesus will come back one day, in exactly the same way as you have seen him go into heaven.'

After completing the plan comes a new beginning

I wonder how the disciples feel after Jesus has ascended into heaven. So much has happened so quickly: Jesus' arrest, death and resurrection, and now he has left them again, to go into heaven. There must be a degree of confusion about the past and about what lies ahead.

It is always good to see a plan come together, to finish a task that has maybe taken a long time to perform. Jesus' return will mark the imminent but ultimate fulfilment of the kingdom: the bringing together of Jesus and his Church – that includes all of us who follow him.

Although Jesus' return signifies the completion of a plan, it also signifies a completely fresh and new beginning, with no more brokenness. It will be a new chapter in our lives, and in God's plan for creation.

What a wonderful thought – especially if we are going through a difficult time living with anxiety or depression: a new beginning to look forward to!

Prayer (looking forward to the ultimate fulfilment of the kingdom):

Loving heavenly Father,
thank you that from the beginning of creation, you have had a wonderful plan that will bring prosperity and blessing.
I (We) look forward to the imminent but ultimate fulfilment of your kingdom, when Jesus returns. Only you know when that will be.
Help me (us) to be ready for that time, so that I (we) may be part of your kingdom, through my (our) relationship with Jesus.
Thank you that when your kingdom reaches its ultimate fulfilment it will not just mark the completion of the plan, but also a new beginning.
Give me (us) the boldness to speak to others about your plan.
In Jesus' name.
Amen.

Finish with the Lord's Prayer.

Pentecost

Be still and quiet: The Holy Spirit – cleansing, transforming and empowering.

Passage to read: Psalm 93.

(Option 1)
Resting in his presence: Sometimes we resist those offers of help from well-meaning people. Sometimes we resist the help of God, through the power of the Holy Spirit. Imagine welcoming someone into your home to help with the cleaning and washing; and then pray:

Heavenly Father, please fill me afresh with the Holy Spirit and help me to allow him freedom in my life to cleanse, transform, guide and strengthen me. In Jesus' name. Amen.

Think for a moment about what it means to allow the Holy Spirit to work in your life – and maybe make some changes.

(Option 2)
Coffee time: Chat over a hot drink about some of the changes you have experienced in your lifetime – some good and some not very good at all. How do you feel about change?

(Option 3)
Make a plan (begin with the prayer – Lord, reveal your plan. Amen): Write a list of any lifestyle changes that you feel you need to make – both in terms of the enablement to live according to God's standards, and as a way of relieving stress

and anxiety and helping to raise your mood. Plan how you are going to put some of those changes in place.

Story to tell (in the author's words):
(Based on Acts 2:1-41)

> The 12 apostles (Matthias having replaced Judas) were all together in a house in Jerusalem, when suddenly they became aware of an unusual noise, similar to that of a violent wind blowing. The noise seemed to sweep into the room in which they were sitting, as well as to fill the whole house. And then what appeared to be tongues of fire followed and came to rest on each of them. As they did so, the apostles were filled with the Holy Spirit. But it wasn't a frightening experience; in fact, there was a feeling of calm and tremendous blessing.
>
> Filled with power from God – the gift that Jesus had promised before his ascension into heaven – the disciples found themselves speaking in different languages. And so, when the 12 went out to talk to the crowd that had gathered in response to hearing the noise, despite the fact that there were people from a number of different countries, everyone was able to hear what the 12 were saying in their own tongue.
>
> 'This is amazing: these men are all Galileans, and yet we are able to hear them in our own languages,' was the response of some in the crowd.
>
> But there were also some sceptics. 'Just listen to them. They've had too much to drink.'

After being filled with the power of the Holy Spirit, Peter discovered he possessed a new boldness, and was inspired to preach to the crowd. He spoke about Jesus:

his life, death and resurrection – and about Jesus being the way to be set free from sin's consequences and to be filled with eternal promise and hope. Peter implored the crowd to repent and be baptised in the name of Jesus, so that they would be forgiven and receive the gift of the indwelling Holy Spirit. And about 3000 people from that crowd became believers.

Progressively transformed into the likeness of Jesus

The work of the indwelling Holy Spirit is to cleanse and progressively transform our lives – so that we become more like Jesus himself. The Holy Spirit also empowers us to live out the Christian life of love and witness. And he gives us spiritual gifts: special abilities to be used to help build the kingdom, and to bring blessing to others – things like preaching, teaching, prophecy, speaking in other tongues and hospitality.

But the Holy Spirit can only do these things in our lives if we allow him the freedom to do so – and if we are willing to make some changes. And it is a lifelong process. Whatever age we might be, the Holy Spirit hasn't finished with us yet!

Prayer (giving thanks for the indwelling Holy Spirit, and asking for both empowerment and spiritual gifts):

Lord Jesus,
thank you for the gift of the Holy Spirit, which you promised to all believers.
Fill me (us) afresh today, and help me (us) to be willing to allow him complete freedom in my life (our lives) – to cleanse, transform, empower and grant me (us) spiritual gifts to be used to bring blessing to others – an ongoing process.
Make me (us) open to putting into place necessary changes.

Help me (us) in my life (our lives) of witness to tell others about you.

And help me (us) to become more like you in the way I (we) live day by day.

I (We) pray that I (we) might see people turning to you in repentance.

Amen.

Finish with the Lord's Prayer.

Harvest

Be still and quiet: Being thankful to God – for the harvest.

Passage to read: Psalm 100.

(Option 1)
Resting in his presence: Spend some time thinking about God's provision through nature: for example, the seed time and the harvest (Genesis 8:22). Remember times when God has faithfully provided for you in other ways. God will not let you down – he is faithful and unchanging. Meditate on that for a few minutes.

(Option 2)
Coffee time: Chat over a hot drink about the harvests of the crops, of the sea and of talents. What do you feel are your talents? Do you feel confident to use them? Sometimes we need to ask a close friend or family member where our abilities lie.

(Option 3)
Make a plan (begin with the prayer – Lord, reveal your plan. Amen): Write a list of your talents and then think about how you can use them more effectively as you seek to serve Jesus – but it must be ways that are going to be achievable.

Story to tell (in the author's words):
(Based on Matthew 13:1-23)

Jesus told this story:

Having prepared the land, a farmer went out to sow some seed. He broadcasted the seed by hand, as usual. And not all of it ended up where it was supposed to go.

Some of the seed fell onto the stony path, where it lay in the heat of the day until passing birds swooped down, picked it up and ate it with great relish.

Some of the seed fell onto the rocky ground, where the soil was extremely shallow. The seed grew quickly and looked really good, until the dry weather came . . . And then it was a different story. Blazing sun meant that the shoots withered quickly, both because the plants had no depth of roots and because the shallow soil dried out so quickly.

Some of the seed fell into the undergrowth, among the thorn bushes. Sure enough it grew, but it wasn't long before the thorns choked the young plants.

But the good news is that some of the seed fell onto the good soil that had been carefully prepared; it grew up well and produced a harvest – a really good one at that!

Later on, Jesus explained to his disciples that the parable was all about how people respond to the message about the kingdom.

He compared the birds picking up the seed from the path with the devil snatching away the message from those who hear it but don't understand it.

The seed that fell onto the rocky ground represents those who initially respond excitedly and positively to the message, but it is a shallow response which only lasts until persecution comes.

The seed that fell among the thorns represents those who allow their initial positive response to be overthrown by the busyness and worries of life.

Of course, the seed that fell onto the good soil represents those who hear the message, understand it, make a commitment to following Jesus and ultimately produce spiritual fruit in their lives – a harvest!

Being fruitful

This parable reminds us to give thanks for the harvest: the harvest of the crops, of the sea and of talents – but also the spiritual harvest. It is intended to make us think about our own response to Scripture and our personal journey with Jesus. Where would you place yourself in this? Are you the path, the rocky soil, the thorny ground, or the soil that produces a harvest?

Whatever our backgrounds or situations, we can all produce spiritual fruit (see Galatians 5:22, 23a).

Prayer (being thankful for the physical and spiritual harvest, and seeking to produce spiritual fruit in our own lives):

Creator God,
thank you for your promise that there will be a seedtime and harvest; and for your ongoing provision to me (us), through your creation.
Thank you for the harvest of the crops, sea and talents.
Thank you that there will be a spiritual harvest.
Help me (us) to be truly committed to following Jesus:

to understand the message of the kingdom; to withstand persecution; not to allow the busyness or worry of life to swamp my (our) faith; and to constantly produce spiritual fruit in my life (our lives) – whatever stage I (we) might be at in my (our) life's journey and whatever my circumstances. I (We) remember those who do not have enough to eat or clean water to drink; and place them into your hands.
In Jesus' name.
Amen.

Finish with the Lord's Prayer.

Remembrance

Be still and quiet: Love – loving our neighbour.

Passage to read: Psalm 107:1-9.

(Option 1)
Resting in his presence: Meditate on self-less love: what constitutes such a love and who has God placed around you to care for you in this way?

(Option 2)
Coffee time: Chat over a hot drink about the danger, the tragic loss of lives, acts of heroism and the sheer destruction associated with situations of warfare. Do you feel that, on the whole, society learns positive lessons from these situations? Qualify your answer.

(Option 3)
Make a plan (begin with the prayer – Lord, reveal your plan. Amen): Choose an appropriate item of clothing on which to wear your poppy for Remembrance. Place it in a buttonhole, or carefully pin it securely. Perhaps you have a neighbour for whom Remembrance is a difficult time. Would you feel able to pop round and offer a word of comfort to them? Does that sound like an achievable goal? Try it!

Story to tell (in the author's words):
(Based on Luke 10:25-37)

One of the most well-known parables of Jesus is probably the parable of the Good Samaritan. You may know the story.

A man was travelling from Jerusalem to Jericho. I have always imagined it to be something of a cross-country journey that took the traveller into deserted hilly areas, where bandits could hide out and attack passing travellers. Sure enough, the man was a victim of robbers: they jumped out and viciously attacked him, took his outer clothing and anything else of any value, and left him seriously injured at the side of the road. His only hope was that someone might come along, take pity on him and offer him help.

The man was convinced that a passing priest would lend a hand – after all, he was a man of God. But the priest passed by without a second glance. I expect he had his reasons why he failed to offer help: maybe he was hurrying to get to an appointment, had other things on his mind or was bound up by religious rules. But there could be no excuse, really!

The next person along the road was a Levite. Surely the Levite would help – or not! He must have been in a hurry as well. Or fearful that the bandits were still lurking, waiting for their next victim to turn up. But some people don't seem to need any excuse not to lend a helping hand or show they care. It can be a sad old world at times, and I'm sure the injured man was beginning to despair of human nature.

The traveller spotted a Samaritan coming towards him. The significance of this was that Jews and Samaritans were not on particularly good terms on the whole. We are led to believe that the injured man, who we assume was a Jew, would not have had high expectations of help from this passer-by. How wrong we can be! Indeed, the Samaritan stopped. He demonstrated great compassion, kindness and generosity as he bandaged the injured man's wounds, lifted him onto his donkey and took him to an inn where he would be safe and cared for – and he even paid for the injured man's stay!

Sharing the love of Jesus

The message is one of loving our neighbour – anyone who is in need. There can be no valid excuse for not exercising Christ-like love in our daily lives. And that love should reach across all barriers of nationality, colour, culture, faith, gender, age, and so on. In his life, and in his death, Jesus is our example of real, unconditional and unselfish love.

During Remembrance we think about, and give thanks for, those who have demonstrated that same kind of selfless love in the fight for peace, as well as those who are still doing so somewhere in the world today – serving in the forces.

We too can live lives demonstrating the same kind of selfless love as Jesus, by being Good Samaritans to those whom we meet day by day – those we know, and those we don't know.

Living with anxiety or depression, you might be asking the question, 'How can I share the love of Jesus with others?' Love can be demonstrated in so many different ways, including in our response to each other. That could be carers, friends, neighbours or family members – demonstrated even through trying circumstances. A word of thanks or encouragement can be so uplifting. Prayer is a wonderful, loving gift to give to others. And there is nothing quite like a smile that says it all!

Prayer (giving thanks for acts of sacrificial love and remembering those who suffer as a result, and asking for the empowerment to love our neighbours):

Lord Jesus,
thank you for your story about helping our neighbours in times of need.
Fill me (us) with your love for others, and help me (us) to make time to stop and help – even if all I am (we are) able to offer is a kind, helpful or encouraging word, a prayer or a smile.
Thank you for those you place around me (us) who care: carers, family, friends, neighbours, colleagues and even strangers.
Thank you for all those who have selflessly sacrificed their lives for the benefit of others – in the fight for peace and in the service of others.
Be with those who grieve for loved ones lost in these ways, and for those who still suffer from injury of body or mind.
In your name.
Amen.

Finish with the Lord's Prayer.

Christmas

Be still and quiet: Jesus – you can't have Christmas without Christ.

Passage to read: Psalm 13.

(Option 1)
Resting in his presence: You might not really feel like celebrating Christmas this year, if you are feeling anxious or particularly low. Close your eyes, and visualise the Son of God as a baby lying in a manger; the angels announcing the occasion to shepherds on the hillside; and later on, the wise men bringing gifts. Peace and goodwill. It's a very different Christmas to that which society celebrates today.

(Option 2)
Coffee time: Chat over a hot drink about your plans for Christmas this year. What does Christmas mean to you? How are you feeling about Christmas fast approaching?

(Option 3)
Make a plan (begin with the prayer – Lord, reveal your plan. Amen): Carefully plan what you are going to do over the Christmas period. Try to make it meaningful but also achievable.

Story to tell (in the author's words):
(Based on Luke 2:8-20)

> Who would have expected it? Would you have expected the first people to be told about the birth

of Jesus to have been a group of shepherds out on the hillside? If it had been now, I am sure some local dignitaries would have been invited (a local MP and maybe an influential church leader) – don't you think? But the place of Jesus' birth was also quite a surprise: the Son of God born in some kind of animal shelter.

Can you imagine the shepherds on the hillside, huddled around a nice warm bonfire, when suddenly the light of the bonfire was swamped by the glory of the Lord shining all around them? I don't know whether that's just like a really bright light? I would imagine it to be something much, much more than that. I use the word 'imagine' quite loosely, because the glory of God is beyond all our imaginations!

First a single angel, then a whole company of angels. And it was to the point: good news, joy, peace and a Saviour born. The angel pointed the shepherds in the right direction to meet with the one person whom the good news was all about: humankind's source of eternal joy and peace – through forgiveness.

After the angels had gone, the shepherds didn't mess about: 'Shall we go and visit, or shall we stay by the fire?' And they didn't get sidetracked about the angelic appearance or even about seeing the glory of God. They hurried off to meet with the baby Jesus for themselves.

After meeting with Jesus, the shepherds went around the neighbourhood telling others about him – and the good news.

Hold on to what really matters at Christmas

Giving presents, eating rich food, bright lights, tinsel, Christmas trees and partying are all associated with Christmas today. Businesses can so often see the 'festive season' as a time to make record profits. For some people it is a time when they end up getting into debt through feeling obliged to spend money they haven't got; and for some it is a time when their loneliness is magnified.

Let's not miss the point this Christmas time: it's actually still about meeting with Jesus, being filled with his peace and joy, receiving forgiveness and knowing eternal hope as a result – and then telling others!

Maybe the festivities of Christmas don't feel as important to you at the moment, while you are feeling anxious or your mood is low. Receive comfort from the true meaning and significance of Christmas.

Prayer (placing Jesus at the centre of Christmas):

Our loving heavenly Father,
thank you for Christmas: the birth of Jesus.
Help me (us) not to allow the bright lights, tinsel and presents to cause me (us) to lose focus on Jesus this Christmas time.
Help me (us) to consider afresh my (our) relationship(s) with him, and increase my (our) faith and commitment.
Let the true meaning of Christmas be proclaimed worldwide this Christmas.
Enable me (us) to feel uplifted by my (our) experience of Jesus at Christmas, even when the festivities might not feel important or be achievable.
In Jesus' name.
Amen.

Finish with the Lord's Prayer.

Men and women of the Old Testament

Adam and Eve

Be still and quiet: Sometimes we make bad choices and disobey God. That has serious consequences, but Jesus can set us free.

Passage to read: Psalm 103:1-6.

(Option 1)
Resting in his presence: Facing choices can be very daunting at times. Say the short prayer that follows and then relax in God's presence for a few minutes and try to let go of the worry.

Heavenly Father, you know the choices I have to make – some of them very significant – please take away the worry and help me to make the right decisions. In Jesus' name. Amen.

(Option 2)
Coffee time: Chat over a hot drink about the different choices we have to make in our lives – some on a daily basis, some very rarely but with life-changing consequences. How easy do you find making choices? Then afterwards, do you worry about whether or not you have made the right choice?

(Option 3)
Make a plan (begin with the prayer – Lord, reveal your plan. Amen): Maybe there are some choices or decisions that you have been putting off for a while. Write down one or two of them and then list the positives and negatives associated with the various options. See if you can make a

selection on that basis. It could be a help for making future choices or decisions.

Story to tell (in the author's words):
(Based on Genesis 3)

> You probably remember the story of Adam and Eve. It comes right at the beginning of the Bible, straight after the account of God creating the world.

> We pick up the story with Adam and Eve settled in the Garden of Eden. Everything was perfect: the garden was a picture of beauty; there were all kinds of amazing animals living in peace and harmony; God had provided a variety of trees, bushes and plants for food; and there was only one rule to be obeyed: 'Don't eat the fruit from the tree in the middle of the garden . . . Don't even touch it – or you will die,' God warned.

> A clear enough warning, you would think! But at the end of the day, God had created Adam and Eve (like us) to have freedom of choice: the opportunity to choose to enter into a close relationship with him from their own free will – or not. Having said that, with freedom of choice can come bad decisions, especially with the devil playing a part in things. Sure enough, the devil turned up in the garden, in the guise of a serpent, and began to spread doubt and lies – as he does.

> 'Are you sure that's what God said?' he asked. 'Perhaps you misunderstood.'

> 'I don't think so,' Eve mumbled, as the doubts began to flood into her mind. 'Well, I suppose I could have heard wrongly or misunderstood.'

There was no misunderstanding, but the fruit did look really good to eat: shiny and ripe. Before long, Eve had picked some for herself and given some to Adam – and they were both tucking in to the fruit. Juice was running down their chins. But before they could even say, 'Delicious!' suddenly they realised the seriousness of what they had done. They had disobeyed God, done the one thing he had told them not to do – and after all the amazing love and generosity that he had showered upon them.

When God arrived in the garden later that day, Adam and Eve were hiding because they were so ashamed about what they had done. Their excuse for hiding was that they had no clothes to wear, but that had never bothered them before.

'Have you been eating the fruit from the tree in the middle of the garden?' God asked.

He knew they had!

Adam pointed accusingly at Eve. 'It was her fault!' Eve blamed the serpent. 'It was his fault!'

But each was responsible for their own actions – as we are, when we deliberately disobey God. And there were consequences: it was the beginning of pain, suffering and death . . . and separation from God.

Set free to enjoy future blessing

Those same consequences apply to us today. But included also in this story is the first prediction of the coming of Jesus – the one who would provide the way for people to be set free from all the consequences of sin. We can be forgiven and restored in our relationship with God, through Jesus – for which we give thanks.

No matter what trials life has placed before us, Genesis 3:15 brings promise of blessing for the eternal future – through the mission of Jesus.

Prayer (giving thanks for forgiveness):

My (Our) loving heavenly Father,
thank you that you love to forgive.
Thank you for Jesus, that through him I (we) can be forgiven.
Forgive me (us) for those bad decisions I (we) have made, which have resulted in me (us) being disobedient to you.
Even when I (we) might be feeling low, help me (us) to remember your promise of eternal blessing: help me (us) to walk close to Jesus day by day, and to be uplifted by the truth of that promise.
Help our modern Western society not to listen to and be taken in by the devil's deceit and tempting.
In Jesus' name.
Amen.

Finish with the Lord's Prayer.

Noah

Be still and quiet: God never forgets us – he is faithful.

Passage to read: Psalm 29.

(Option 1)
Resting in his presence: There is a saying that goes something like: 'out of sight, out of mind'. Do you sometimes feel forgotten by others when you are unable to get out? For a few moments focus on a difficult, sad or lonely time in your life when you have been particularly aware of God's faithfulness to you. He will never forget you.

(Option 2)
Coffee time: Chat over a hot drink about ways in which we can experience the faithfulness of God in our lives. Knowing that God is faithful is relatively easy; applying that knowledge and gaining confidence from it is sometimes quite difficult – especially when we feel anxious or our mood is low. What do you think?

(Option 3)
Make a plan (begin with the prayer – Lord, reveal your plan. Amen)**:** Choose a picture of a favourite pet from the past to look at; or if you still have a pet, spend some time playing with it, cuddling it or just sitting together. Pets can be very therapeutic – they can also be very faithful. Let this remind you of God's faithfulness at all times and in all situations.

Story to tell (in the author's words):
(Based on Genesis 6–9)

Imagine how Noah felt when God instructed him to build a boat big enough to house his own family and two of every living creature and bird (male and female) – as well as food. It wasn't as if Noah had any experience of being a boat builder – as far as we know. The big boat was to be called an ark.

The situation was that God was aggrieved about the amount of wickedness that had arisen in the world at that time. Noah and his family were the only people who were still obedient to God, and prepared to listen to him. God's plan was to give creation a fresh start by flooding the earth. The ark would be the only place of safety!

Building such a craft would have been a huge job, much more so than building a rowing boat or a coracle. The ark was to have three decks. Huge amounts of heavy cypress wood would be needed in order to build it, and large quantities of pitch would be required to seal it from the water. And I dare say poor Noah and his family would have had to suffer considerable amounts of scorn and ridicule while pursuing the task.

Some people ask the question: How could the Noah family possibly have rounded up all the different animals to put onto the ark? But the Bible is quite explicit: the animals came on their own, because God sent them!

And so, the boat was completed; Noah, his family, and all the animals were on board, ready for the flood. Imagine how the boat builder must have felt: 'I wonder when it's going to rain.'

And so the waiting began.

But sure enough, the rain came in abundance, and also springs opened up from under the ground. This continued for 40 days and nights. Thankfully, the large vessel rose up in the water and floated majestically over the waves.

Scripture tells us that all through the flood, God never forgot Noah, his family and their precious cargo. Eventually the water subsided, the land dried up and God told Noah that it was safe to disembark.

It was a fresh new start for creation as God led Noah and his party onto the safety of dry land. And God promised that he would never flood the earth in the same way again – and as a sign of his promise he sent the rainbow.

Never forgotten

The Bible is full of amazing promises with eternal potential, including finding a place of safety through a personal relationship with Jesus. The rainbow still reminds us of God's faithfulness in fulfilling his promises. And, of course, when we live in faith and obedience to God, he will never leave or forget us ... Not even while living with anxiety or depression, when it is easy to feel isolated, forgotten or left out.

Prayer (thanking God for his faithfulness):

Our loving heavenly Father,
thank you for your faithfulness to me (us): whatever my (our) situation is, and whatever age I (we) might be, you never forget me (us) or abandon me (us).

Thank you for all the wonderful promises in the Bible; and for the sign of the rainbow, which reminds me (us) that you never break your promises.

Reinforce my (our) trust in you.

As I (we) live with anxiety (depression), help me (us) not to feel left out or forgotten by people.

I (We) pray that others might turn to you and claim your promises.

In Jesus' name.

Amen.

Finish with the Lord's Prayer.

Joseph

Be still and quiet: We don't always see the bigger picture when we ask, 'Why suffering?'

Passage to read: Psalm 80.

(Option 1)
Resting in his presence: Think about times in your life when God has brought a good outcome from a difficult or tragic situation. Try to draw some reassurance from that, as you spend some time resting in God's presence. Listen to what he might be saying to you.

(Option 2)
Coffee time: Chat over a hot drink about whether or not you believe in coincidence – or is it God's hand at work? How does that make you feel about some of the more difficult times you have experienced?

(Option 3)
Make a plan (begin with the prayer – Lord, reveal your plan. Amen)**:** Maybe you are at a stage in your anxiety or depression when you are able to look back and realise that you have grown stronger or learned something during this experience that could be useful to you – or to others. Perhaps this will influence your plan for the immediate (or more distant) future.

Story to tell (in the author's words):
(Based on Genesis 37–50)

We tend to associate Joseph with a brightly coloured coat. The story goes like this:

> Joseph was highly favoured by his father, Jacob. That's why Jacob gave Joseph a brightly coloured coat, when Joseph was 17 years old.
>
> Today's young people would probably exclaim, 'It's absolutely hideous, Dad! You needn't think I'm going to wear that!'
>
> But for Joseph and his brothers it made the statement, 'This is my favourite son!'
>
> It was unfortunate for the young man because it further damaged what was already a rocky relationship with his older brothers. And to make matters worse, Joseph had two dreams, which he felt appropriate to share with the whole family. The first one involved sheaves of corn in a harvest field; and the second was about the sun, moon and 11 stars. In context, both were suggestive that one day Joseph's parents and brothers would be bowing down to him. Joseph believed this to be a word from God – to be fulfilled in the future. His family believed it to be conceit to the utmost extent. Needless to say, the relationships became even more strained.
>
> From such a privileged position, things very quickly deteriorated. Joseph's brothers were so angry that they sold Joseph into slavery, and then came up with some cock-and-bull story to relay to their poor father. 'Look, Dad, we found his brightly coloured coat – well, at least, we think

it was his. He must have been eaten by some ferocious animal. How awful!'

Their father believed what they said and sobbed, 'You're right, my sons: it is his coat – there's no doubt about that. What a terrible thing to happen!'

But while Joseph's dad was mourning his death, the boy was already on his way to Egypt to enter the household of Potiphar.

After a time of prosperity, Joseph ended up in prison following false accusations made against him. It was while he was in there that he discovered a God-given gift of interpreting dreams. In time, this gift enabled Joseph's release from prison in order to interpret Pharaoh's dreams. These dreams were of great significance, as they involved a forthcoming serious famine.

'There will be seven years of plenty, followed by seven years of failed crops,' Joseph explained. 'During the first seven years, food must be put aside for the second seven years. Someone needs to be appointed to organise this.'

Pharaoh selected Joseph as the right man for the job.

And to cut a long story short, years later Joseph's family arrived in Egypt to try and buy food during the famine. They bowed down before Joseph who, by this time, had become very important in those parts. Eventually they were all reunited after Joseph explained who hc was, and Pharaoh invited the whole family to come and live in Egypt, where there was still food. Of course, a lot of forgiveness had to take place.

It's not a coincidence

Some might say that Joseph's is a story of coincidences, a lucky outcome. But remember Joseph's dreams in his youth, when God tells him that one day the rest of the family will bow down to him? God allows Joseph to go through times of suffering in order to save his family from inevitable death – and more than that, to enable God's chosen people to survive.

We can often look back over our life experiences and realise that in actual fact God's hand has been in those so-called 'coincidences'!

Prayer (asking for faith and strength in times of suffering):

Almighty God,
you know the bigger picture, and you know why there are times when I (we) go through difficult experiences and periods of suffering.
You know that, for some, anxiety or depression is a particular struggle, often leading to isolation.
Be with me (us), especially during such times. Increase my (our) faith and strength to enable me (us) to carry on despite the difficulties, loneliness and suffering.
Be with others who are going through anxiety or depression.
Thank you for those glimpses of the bigger picture when I (we) look back over my life and realise that those coincidences were your hand at work.
In Jesus' name.
Amen.

Finish with the Lord's Prayer.

Moses

Be still and quiet: God's protection – especially when we feel vulnerable.

Passage to read: Psalm 91:1-8.

(Option 1)
Resting in his presence: Perhaps you are feeling vulnerable today. Think about a time when you felt God's protection: for example, as you came safely through a dangerous situation. Meditate on Matthew 28:20 where Jesus promises never to leave those who follow him.

(Option 2)
Coffee time: Chat over a hot drink about what it means to be safe. Talk about times and situations in which you have felt unsafe.

(Option 3)
Make a plan (begin with the prayer – Lord, reveal your plan. Amen)**:** Choose one of the following phrases that best sums up how you are feeling, and complete it:

- I feel vulnerable all the time, because . . .

- I feel vulnerable some of the time, because . . .

- I do not feel vulnerable, because . . .

Seek some practical ways of avoiding or coping better with those situations that make you feel unsafe or vulnerable – and how to implement them.

Story to tell (in the author's words):
(Based on Exodus 1:1–2:10)

The story of Moses began in Egypt. The Israelites had moved there to escape a severe famine during the time of Joseph. They had settled down well, multiplied and become extremely prosperous. Under a new king (or pharaoh), the Egyptians put the Israelites into slavery, treating them ruthlessly and without mercy. The king even gave orders for any male Israelite babies to be killed. But God knew the terrible things that were happening, and in his love and compassion he had a plan to set the Israelites free. The plan began with God choosing Moses to lead the Israelites out of Egypt. But first the baby Moses had to be protected against any harm resulting from the king's orders concerning male Israelite babies.

Moses' parents managed to hide him for three months but, as you can imagine, as the baby grew older, it became more and more difficult to conceal him. Led by God, Moses' mother knew just what to do. She found a basket large enough to place the child in and made it waterproof by coating it with tar and pitch. The idea was to float the child in the little basket, near to where the king's daughter used to bathe each day. Perhaps she would feel sorry for the baby Moses and save him from being killed. Moses' older sister watched as her mother placed the basket among the reeds at the side of the River Nile.

Sure enough, as usual, the beautiful young princess came down to the river's edge to bathe.

She was enjoying the water when she heard a baby crying. Following the sound, she eventually found the child. God had his hand on the situation: indeed, it was all part of his bigger plan. The princess felt sorry for Moses and wanted to keep him.

Moses' sister hurried over. 'I know a lady who would look after him for you while he is small.'

The princess was pleased with the suggestion. 'Go and fetch her. I will pay her to nurse him until he gets a little older, and then I will bring him up as my own son.'

So the little girl went to fetch Moses' mother, who was able to take the child home again and care for him until he was old enough to go and live at the palace with the princess.

God's protection

So what can we learn from this story?

In isolation, it is a story about God's protection of Moses during a difficult time. But if we are to include the wider story of Moses, it is about the protection of the Israelites. And its application to us today is that God will protect us – even through the most difficult situations. (For the wider story of Moses, see the book of Exodus.)

There can be feelings of vulnerability while living with anxiety or depression, linked with things like losses of confidence, self-esteem and motivation. At such times we can prayerfully seek God's protection.

Prayer (asking that God will protect us when we are feeling vulnerable):

Almighty God,
thank you that you are a powerful God.
Protect me (us), even in the most difficult situations when I am (we are) feeling really vulnerable.
Be with others as they too face difficult or dangerous times.
In Jesus' name.
Amen.

Finish with the Lord's Prayer.

Ruth

Be still and quiet: People who care – depending on others.

Passage to read: Psalm 105:1-22.

(Option 1)
Resting in his presence: Spend some time in an attitude of thankfulness for those dependable people whom God has placed around you for a time like this.

(Option 2)
Coffee time: Chat over a hot drink about what it feels like to depend on others. Talk about some of the things for which you might be dependent on others.

(Option 3)
Make a plan (begin with the prayer – Lord, reveal your plan. Amen)**:** Choose a photograph, an object in the house or even a number on your telephone that reminds you of someone you depend on. Maybe there are others that have expressed a willingness to help at this time; but you have not taken up their offer. Sometimes we need help from others to enable us to cope and maintain our independence. Consider carefully if you need to ask for further assistance from those God has placed around you.

Story to tell (in the author's words):
(Based on Ruth 1–4)

> Parts of Ruth's story are extremely sad and traumatic, yet at the same time it is a romantic love story. But the story begins with Naomi.
>
> As a result of a famine in Judah, Naomi, her husband (Elimelech) and their two sons (Mahlon and Kilion) went to live in Moab. It wasn't their choice; it was a matter of life or death. The little family were determined to make the best of the situation, but they suffered terrible misfortune. Before long, Elimelech died quite suddenly and unexpectedly. Despite the family's grief, still determined to be positive, the two boys met two local girls – Orpah and Ruth – and got married to them. But still more tragedy hit the family when Mahlon and Kilion died. The only good bit of news that eventually came their way was that, at long last, there was food again in Judah.
>
> Naomi and the two girls prepared to journey back home – well, home for Naomi. Back to Judah.
>
> However, as they set out on the long journey, Naomi turned to Orpah and Ruth and lovingly said, 'Go back to your own homes and families, and I will return to mine. You have been good to me in many ways, but now you must think of your own futures.'
>
> The two daughters-in-law became very emotional as they hugged Naomi. They had become very close to each other during the time they had been together as a family.

'Don't be silly. We won't leave you. We'll come with you to Judah,' they argued.

But the wise old lady wouldn't have it. 'I have nothing to offer you. I don't have any more sons for you to marry. Go home, and you will find someone else with whom you can start a new life.'

Orpah hugged Naomi again. And a tearful 'goodbye' followed as the young lady walked away. Ruth, on the other hand, was determined that nothing would separate her from her friend and mother-in-law.

'Please don't send me away. I want to come with you wherever you go. I want your God to be my God. I want your people to be my people. My desire is that only death will eventually part us,' Ruth declared.

Naomi was surprised. Ruth probably surprised herself a little, with such a declaration of total commitment. What could Naomi say in reply? And so the two women returned to Bethlehem in Judah to pick up the pieces. Well . . . so they thought. In actual fact, it was more like a fresh new start.

While working hard to provide food for herself and Naomi, Ruth fell in love with a young farmer called Boaz. One of the conditions of the young couple being able to get married was that Boaz had to buy the land that had belonged to Elimelech, to keep it in the family. Of course, he was more than happy to do that. So Boaz and Ruth got married and then had a son called Obed (who became grandfather to King David). What a wonderful ending to the story!

Learning to depend on others

Ruth's story is crucial to the ancestry into which Jesus is born. It is a story about redemption: just as Boaz enables Ruth to be free to marry him, through paying the price for Elimelech's land, Jesus has paid the penalty for our sin, so that we might be free to enter into an eternal and personal relationship with him (and experience his forgiveness through that relationship). And it is a story about commitment and hope, and illustrates that we sometimes need to learn to depend on others in difficult times – for example, times of sickness, frailty or old age.

Prayer (to learn to depend on others – especially God):

Almighty God,
thank you that I (we) can depend on you, and that in times of need you also place others around me (us) on whom I (we) can depend. But it can sometimes be difficult to overcome my (our) feelings of independence. Help me (us) to do that.
Thank you that through Jesus paying the penalty for sin, he has made it possible for all of humankind to enter into an eternal, personal relationship with him – and thus with you and the Holy Spirit – and to be forgiven.
Help me (us) to repentantly and in faith depend on Jesus as my (our) Lord and Saviour.
Be with all those who have had to learn to depend on others, in different ways and for different reasons.
In Jesus' name.
Amen.

Finish with the Lord's Prayer.

David

Be still and quiet: Defeating those things that seem very big and frightening in our lives, with God's help; finding the enablement to live our lives when facing those things.

Passage to read: Psalm 1.

(Option 1)
Resting in his presence: Pray the following short prayer, placing difficult or fearful situations into God's hands. And then rest in God's presence for a few minutes.

Heavenly Father, please help me to win the victory over those situations in my life currently that seem to be so big and frightening. In Jesus' name.
Amen.

(Option 2)
Coffee time: Chat over a hot drink about some of the more illogical and maybe even humorous fears that you have. Then (if you feel able) share a fear that is more significant in your life.

(Option 3)
Make a plan (begin with the prayer – Lord, reveal your plan. Amen): Write a list of those things that make you fearful; and consider which of them are rational fears, and how they can be reduced or managed in such a way that life can carry on despite them.

Story to tell (in the author's words):
(Based on 1 Samuel 17)

David was one of those people who went through childhood appearing to be no one special – and I don't mean that in a contemptuous way. He was a shepherd boy, which would have been looked upon as a very ordinary job at the time. I suppose the first real surprise came when Samuel visited and announced that God had chosen the young shepherd boy to be the next king . . . but in the meantime, life just carried on as normal.

David's first real break was when he was summoned to King Saul because of his ability to play the harp. His attendants thought it might help when the king was in a bad humour. Saul took to the young man, requesting that he should become part of the staff in the royal palace. And so, after that, David would spend some of his time with King Saul and some back at home caring for his father's sheep.

All was well until the Philistines turned up – with no good intentions towards the Israelites. There was one particular warrior in their midst, who was called Goliath. He was really tall and strong, and quite 'in your face'.

'Come and fight me,' he challenged. 'Nominate someone, and if they kill me, the Philistines will be your subjects. And if not,' he grinned, 'you will become our subjects.'

Goliath had that intimidating manner. Everyone was afraid of this huge man. He made his challenge twice a day for 40 days, and nobody was brave enough to face him.

About this time it happened that his father, Jesse, asked David to go and visit his brothers who were in Saul's army, to take them a food hamper, and then to report back how they were. Not by chance, I am sure! To everyone's surprise, young David volunteered to go and fight Goliath. I expect there was some laughter and scornful remarks made before David was taken seriously. Saul tried to get David to wear a fine suit of armour, but it was not what the brave young shepherd boy was used to. All he needed was his sling, a few small pebbles and God with him.

Goliath was filled with anger, insulted that the Israelites would send a shepherd boy out to fight him. He used some choice words as he literally looked down on David.

But David refused to be intimidated as he confidently replied, 'God is on my side.'

The battle was soon over, as the mighty Philistine warrior fell to the floor after one of the pebbles dealt him a fatal blow. The young man David knew that the victory belonged to God.

David went on to be a great king. The battle with Goliath was just the beginning of his life of trust in God. If we were to look at the wider story of David we would discover that he had to face many big and frightening situations during his rule as king. (For the wider story of David, see 1 Samuel 16–31; the book of 2 Samuel; and 1 Kings 1:1–2:12.)

Coping with those things in our lives that appear to be 'big and frightening'

God will help us to deal with the things that seem very big and frightening in our lives: those difficult decisions we have to make; times of acute sadness or regret; periods of sickness or suffering in our lives or the lives of those we are close to; getting old; failing health; not coping; fears; low mood and anxieties . . . Whatever those big and frightening things might be in our lives, when we include God and ask for his help and sustenance, he will either overcome them or give us the strength to carry on despite our circumstances. Either way, we share in his victory!

Prayer (for help to face the things that seem very big and frightening in our lives):

Mighty God,
thank you that I am (we are) not on my (our) own as I (we) face those things that seem very big and frightening in my life (our lives).
You know the things that I am (we are) struggling with at the moment: maybe difficult decisions I (we) have to make; times of acute sadness or regret; periods of sickness or suffering in my life (our lives) or the lives of those I am (we are) close to; those fears; low mood and all the anxieties.
(You may add your own specific situation(s) and struggle(s) you battle with – and/or those of others.)
Strengthen and sustain me (us): help me (us) either to overcome those things that seem very big and frightening in my life (our lives); or, at least, enable me (us) to carry on despite my (our) circumstances.
In Jesus' name.
Amen.

Finish with the Lord's Prayer.

Jonah

Be still and quiet: God is everywhere – we can't run away from him!

Passage to read: Psalm 91:9-16.

(Option 1)
Resting in his presence: Close your eyes and visualise someone physically trying to run away from God; that person might be you – and you will know why and in what way. Then picture that person coming to a standstill – no more running. Try to feel the relief as that person turns to face God with a willingness to enter into God's plan (Jeremiah 29:11).

(Option 2)
Coffee time: Chat over a hot drink about what it means to try to run away from God. Give some hypothetical examples. Talk about anything you might be trying to run away from at the present time, and why. God could be in your list.

(Option 3)
Make a plan (begin with the prayer – Lord, reveal your plan. Amen): Plan a run or a walk for later on in the day: the venue is your choice – it could be a favourite beauty spot or around the garden. Exercise is valuable to physical and mental health; but while you are exercising remember that you cannot run away from God. Consider if you are trying to do that in any way.

Story to tell (in the author's words):
(Based on Jonah 1–4)

I wonder if you have ever tried to run away from anyone.

Having been called by God to go and preach against the wickedness in Nineveh – a job that didn't really appeal very much – Jonah thought he could outrun God. He hastened down to Joppa.

'Can you take me to Tarshish?' he pleaded as he scrambled on board a boat that was moored in the docks.

The old sea captain nodded. 'It'll cost you.'

Jonah paid his fare and then found somewhere comfortable to lie down and have a sleep. He was convinced that before long he would be out of reach of God. How wrong you can be!

It wasn't very long at all before the wind got up, the waves got bigger, and the little boat began to be tossed precariously in the rough sea – so much so that everyone feared for their lives. Well, everyone except Jonah, because he was still fast asleep.

'Get up and start praying harder than you've ever done before,' the captain commanded as he poked the sleeping man.

Jonah woke up with a start. 'What's all the fuss about?'

Suddenly the boat rolled precariously, throwing the two men across the floor. 'That's what the fuss is all about!'

It was decided to cast lots to see whose fault this horrendous storm could be. Of course, Jonah drew the short straw. 'What have you been up to, that has made your God so angry?'

At long last, Jonah realised that it was impossible to run away from God, so he gave the sailors the instruction, 'Throw me overboard and save yourselves.'

He probably didn't expect to be taken up on that – in fact, he wasn't to start with – but then out of desperation the crew picked up poor Jonah and tossed him into the raging sea.

The sea grew calm. Jonah didn't have to swim too far, because God sent a huge fish to swallow him – and keep him safe. It smelled a bit inside the fish and wasn't particularly comfortable, but it gave Jonah time to really focus on God – and to do some more praying. In fact, he did lots of praying!

Three long days and three long nights later, the big fish vomited Jonah out onto the beach; and once again came the call of God: 'Go to Nineveh.'

This time Jonah obeyed, and passed on God's message: 'God's not at all happy with you lot; you've been very wicked.'

To Jonah's surprise, everyone repented, and God forgave them. And the story finished with Jonah not really understanding the depth of God's love, compassion and forgiveness – until God gave him a little visual demonstration.

We can't run away from God

The story of Jonah is about a God of love, compassion and forgiveness; but it is also about a God we can't run away from, however much we might try. Because God is everywhere!

Some people spend their whole lives trying to run away from God.

Prayer (thanking God for his love, compassion and forgiveness, and the fact that he is everywhere):

Heavenly Father,
thank you that wherever I am (we are), I am (we are) always in your presence – I (we) can never run away from you.
Thank you for your love, compassion and forgiveness.
Help me (us), like the people from Nineveh, to turn to you in repentance and trust – if I (we) haven't already.
If I am (we are) trying to run away from you, like Jonah at the beginning of the story, help me (us) to stop running – and to be obedient to your calling and will.
And I (we) pray for others who might be running away from you at this time.
In Jesus' name.
Amen.

Finish with the Lord's Prayer.

PART THREE: NEW TESTAMENT

People who meet with Jesus

The tempter

Be still and quiet: Trusting in the truth of the Bible – God's word.

Passage to read: Psalm 33:1-11.

(Option 1)
Resting in his presence: Choose a favourite verse of Scripture, which has a particular significance in your life – and meditate on it. Focus on the comfort, strength, guidance or promise that it offers.

(Option 2)
Coffee time: Chat over a hot drink about people you have trusted in your life. What has made them trustworthy? Maybe there have been people who have let you down in different ways. How does that make you feel?

(Option 3)
Make a plan (begin with the prayer – Lord, reveal your plan. Amen): Choose a favourite Bible passage. Why is it such a favourite? Maybe it brings back memories of a special time in your life. Perhaps it has been a great comfort or help to you on a variety of occasions. It might offer great comfort and hope to you at the present time.

Story to tell (in the author's words):
(Based on Matthew 4:1-11)

> After Jesus' baptism, the Holy Spirit led him into the desert to have some quiet time with God, to prepare for his forthcoming ministry. For 40 days and nights Jesus fasted, as he spent time in prayer and thought, listening to what the Father was saying to him. We can imagine Jesus being really hungry by the end of this time, and that's when the tempter popped in to try to lead Jesus away from the plans and purposes of God – because that is what he does!
>
> 'I expect you're feeling peckish now,' the tempter observed. 'Easily solved, though. You could turn those stones into bread – and have a real feast.'
>
> But Jesus wasn't to be taken in: he pointed the devil to the Scriptures where it says quite emphatically that we need more than physical food to satisfy – we need the word of God (the Bible).
>
> The tempter took Jesus to Jerusalem, to the highest point of the temple. 'Talking of the Scriptures, it says that the angels will protect you. Prove to me that you really are the Son of God by jumping off here, and we'll see who comes to save you.'
>
> Jesus pointed the devil to another part of the Scriptures where it tells us not to put God to the test.
>
> 'Okay!' the tempter announced as he took Jesus to a very high mountain and pointed to all the cities, towns and villages scattered around. 'Look! If you would bow down and worship me – do things my way – then all this could be yours.'
>
> Once again Jesus pointed the devil to the Scriptures where it tells us to worship and serve

God – and no one else. Jesus commanded the devil to go. With that, the devil left and angels came to minister to Jesus.

Find strength and guidance from God's word

This is a warning to us. The tempter is never far away, and he will always tempt us when we are at our weakest: hungry, thirsty, lonely, stressed, tired, anxious, discouraged, upset . . . But it's not wrong to be tempted: it only becomes sin if we give in to that temptation. Remember, Jesus is our guide and example: we too must look to the truth of the Bible when we face temptation.

Some people collect stamps; others collect teapots . . . and still others accumulate verses of Scripture in their memories during the course of their life's journey – that is such a valuable resource to have!

Prayer (giving thanks for the truth and guidance of the Bible, and asking for understanding):

My (Our) loving heavenly Father,

thank you for the truth of the Bible: as well as being full of wonderful promises and guidance, it has the answers for when I am (we are) faced with difficult decisions and find myself (ourselves) in situations of temptation.

Thank you for those precious and useful verses that I (we) have been able to recall or turn to at different times in my life (our lives).

Help me (us) through the power of the Holy Spirit to read and understand more of the Bible, and to put into practice those things that I (we) learn.

Strengthen me (us) as I (we) face temptation – help me (us) to say 'No!'
Be with and speak to those who are struggling to find answers at this time.
In Jesus' name.
Amen.

Finish with the Lord's Prayer.

Some fishermen

Be still and quiet: Fishing for people – witnessing to and sharing our own story with others; what Jesus has done for me!

Passage to read: Psalm 30.

(Option 1)
Resting in his presence: Think about what you might like to say to others about your personal walk with Jesus. It might be helpful to jot some notes down.

(Option 2)
Coffee time: Chat over a hot drink about different ways in which we can share the good news of forgiveness, a second chance and eternal hope available through Jesus. How do those aspects of the Christian faith make you feel?

(Option 3)
Make a plan (begin with the prayer – Lord, reveal your plan. Amen)**:** Choose a favourite story, parable or verse from the Bible that has always encouraged you in your faith. Decide what aspects of it were particularly significant to you in the past. Prayerfully seek strength and encouragement from it, in your spiritual life at the present time.

Story to tell (in the author's words):
(Based on Matthew 4:18-22)

> I guess it would not have been an unfamiliar sight
> while walking beside the Sea of Galilee to see fishermen

making repairs on their boats, preparing their nets and setting out to fish. But it was no accident or coincidence that Jesus had set out to walk along that path on this particular day. He had started out on a mission, with the aim of finding four particular fishermen to ask them a very special question.

We can imagine the scene: a bright, warm, sunshiny day. The fishermen were busy preparing to go out fishing, unaware of passers-by. Jesus was walking along, enjoying the views across the water, feeling the sun on his face, watching all the different fishermen about their business, and listening to the hungry birds always looking for scraps of fish. Perhaps there was a fishiness about the air. But remember, Jesus was on a mission to look for four particular fishermen.

At last he spotted the first two: Simon Peter and his brother Andrew. They were already out on the lake casting their net with the skill and expertise of true fishermen. Jesus watched for a few moments before shouting across the water to them.

'Will you follow me, and then I will teach you how to fish people into the kingdom?'

Maybe Simon Peter and Andrew had met with Jesus before, but it was still a big ask: after all, he was asking them to give up their business – their livelihood. They could have been forgiven for requesting time to think about it – or at least, to make arrangements. But there was none of that: in came the net, they sailed the little boat back to the shore and followed Jesus without a second thought.

A little further along the shore, Jesus saw James and his brother John in their boat getting their net ready, with their father Zebedee. Jesus called the two boys, and immediately they walked away from the family business to follow him.

Following Jesus and then sharing our story with others

That's quite something: to leave everything and immediately follow Jesus. It's about relationship and priority. Jesus wants to be in a personal relationship with each one of us today, and he wants us to make it a priority to follow him. Following Jesus means following his teaching and guidance, striving to be more like him and having a close relationship with him – walking with him day by day.

Maybe Jesus has been the main priority in your life for many years now – or maybe not.

I think our priorities often change as we get older or in times of illness (physical or mental): material objects that may have seemed so important in the past suddenly don't seem as important any more. Perhaps now is the time to consider entering into that relationship with Jesus – if you haven't done so already.

However, the essence of this story is really about telling other people the good news: of forgiveness, a second chance and eternal hope available through Jesus. When we have entered into a personal relationship with Jesus ourselves, we should talk to others about our experience, as well as about what the Bible teaches, to help lead them closer to Jesus (part of the process of fishing people into the kingdom). And there's a lot of fishing still to be done in the world around us: people who need to hear about Jesus. Those people are often closer to home than we might imagine, and it is something we can all do.

Prayer (having the courage to speak to others about Jesus):

Lord Jesus,
thank you for your offer of forgiveness, a second chance and eternal hope through a relationship with you.
Help me (us) to walk closer to you each day of my life (our lives): to know you better, to trust you more, to listen to your guidance and to strive to become increasingly like you.
Give me (us) the courage and the right words to say when I (we) have the opportunity to speak to others about you, and my (our) relationship with you.
Make me a fisher (us fishers) of men.
Fill me (us) afresh with the power of your Holy Spirit to do that.
Prepare the hearts and minds of those to whom I (we) will speak about you.
In your name.
Amen.

Finish with the Lord's Prayer.

Matthew

Be still and quiet: Called to follow Jesus – making an immediate response.

Passage to read: Psalm 42.

(Option 1)
Resting in his presence: As you spend a few minutes resting peacefully in God's presence, think about your response to Jesus' calling to follow him: what was it like – or are you still undecided?

(Option 2)
Coffee time: Chat over a hot drink about the cost of following Jesus – things like time, change of lifestyle and maybe even financial costs. What do you feel is the greatest cost to you at the moment? Maybe you are struggling to find the motivation to really commit to following Jesus at this time, as a result of living with anxiety or depression. It might be helpful to talk about it.

(Option 3)
Make a plan (begin with the prayer – Lord, reveal your plan. Amen)**:** Seek Jesus' guidance for your immediate future.

Story to tell (in the author's words):
(Based on Matthew 9:9-13)

> It was just another day for Matthew as he sat at his tax-collecting booth, collecting taxes. In reality,

it probably hadn't been his first choice of jobs, although it did pay quite well. But being renowned for dishonesty and working on behalf of the Romans didn't make the tax collectors of the time very popular with the Jews.

We can imagine Matthew dealing with a queue of disillusioned people on this occasion, who were angry at being exploited once again. Already his day had probably been coloured by resentment from his customers. But then he looked up to see Jesus' loving face smiling at him.

'Good afternoon, Matthew.' Enough to brighten anyone's day. 'I've come to invite you to follow me.'

I would have expected a few questions to be asked. But no: Matthew jumped up excitedly and with determination. He pulled the shutters down, banged the door behind him and hurried over to where Jesus was standing.

'Here I am! Let's go then!'

Later that day, Matthew threw a dinner party. All sorts of people were there, including tax collector friends and some other people who did not win the approval of the local community.

The Pharisees were never far away from Jesus, and on this particular evening they approached some of his disciples – to criticise. 'What's going on here: tax collectors, people of dubious character, and Jesus in their midst? Why? Why can't your teacher find some better friends to mix with?'

Jesus overheard their scathing comments. 'People who are ill need to see the doctor; wouldn't you agree?' They nodded. 'Well, my ministry is to those who are spiritually sick. I can reach and help those who know they have disobeyed God; but not those who like to think they're perfect.'

The Pharisees probably missed the point on that occasion.

Making a response to Jesus

What Jesus is saying is that we have all done things wrong, fallen short of God's standards – and that's what his mission is all about. But in order to receive Jesus' forgiveness, a fresh start and hope for eternity, we need to follow him in the knowledge and acceptance that we have all sinned. Those who think that they are living perfect lives are deluded, and are not in a position of being able to benefit from the salvation Jesus offers.

In the story, Matthew responds immediately and decisively to Jesus' invitation to follow him. What is your response? Remember there is no age limit!

Prayer (that we might make a positive response to Jesus):

Dear Lord Jesus,
thank you that your mission is to sinners – that's everyone!
Thank you for the opportunity to follow you: to be forgiven, to be given a second chance and to be filled with eternal hope.
Help me (us) to respond positively to your invitation to follow you, and not to put off that decision.
Help me (us) to walk closer to you each day.
I (We) pray for those who still refuse to turn to you.
In your name.
Amen.

Finish with the Lord's Prayer.

Mary and Martha

Be still and quiet: Being still – and listening to Jesus.

Passage to read: Psalm 46.

(Option 1)
Resting in his presence: Maybe you find it difficult to be still and quiet in God's presence – to listen to him – seeking things like guidance and encouragement. Think about the importance of doing so, and then try it afresh for a few minutes.

(Option 2)
Coffee time: Chat over a hot drink about when your best time is and where your best place is to be still and quiet in God's presence. Or perhaps you have a fear that the stillness and quiet will open up all kinds of painful memories from the past. Elaborate on how you feel.

(Option 3)
Make a plan (begin with the prayer – Lord, reveal your plan. Amen): Choose a place in the house or garden where you can sit quietly with Jesus, for 10 or 15 minutes (if it is somewhere different from the place where your act of worship is taking place, you can take your hot drinks with you). Listen to what Jesus has to say to you – it might be, 'Rest in my presence.' Maybe you need to do this more often.

Story to tell (in the author's words):
(Based on Luke 10:38-42)

> Martha had always been a busy sort of person.
> She couldn't bear to see a job that needed doing
> around the house and not attend to it. And when
> she had people round to entertain, she just wanted
> everything to be perfect for them – well, as near to
> perfect as anyone could manage. The house had to be
> spotless, warm, comfortable and inviting. The food
> had to be fresh, tasty and plentiful. And nothing
> would ever be too much trouble.
>
> On this particular occasion Martha had invited
> Jesus and his disciples to come round. Despite all the
> preparations beforehand, as soon as they arrived she
> began to bustle around, making sure that everything
> was okay for her guests. It wasn't that she wanted to
> show off, or that she was obsessive about household
> chores; she just wanted it to be nice and welcoming.
>
> As Martha hurried around, she became irritated
> by her sister Mary who could have been helping
> but had chosen to sit near Jesus' feet, listening to
> his wonderful stories about the kingdom. Martha
> thought to herself, 'Doesn't she think I would like to
> have sat down in Jesus' company for a few minutes
> as well? But someone has to do the work.' In the
> end, Martha could stand it no longer: fuming, she
> hurried over to Jesus.
>
> 'Will you tell my sister to come and help me,
> please – she has left me to do everything. Now I am
> worn out.'

I am sure Jesus will have smiled warmly and answered with compassion and not as a reprimand for his dear friend. 'Martha, it is not good for you to put yourself under so much stress, worrying about unnecessary things. Mary has made the better choice; one which I cannot go against.'

Being still and quiet in Jesus' presence

I am sure we have sympathy for Martha and her good intentions; maybe we associate with her busyness in our own lives. We live in a very busy world, where even leisure time at home seems to be filled with phone calls, emails, the internet, radio, TV . . . maybe even carers, family members, friends or neighbours dropping in. Many of those are things that have some good and positive benefits, but where in the midst of all the noise and busyness do we find time for God? Time when we are still and quiet with Jesus, to listen to what he has to say to us and to rest in his presence?

Martha is filled with good intentions, but good intentions are not enough: we need to do the right thing. Mary has made the better choice – to be still and quiet as she learns from Jesus!

It can be difficult to find the time or inclination to be still and quiet in Jesus' presence – but it is so important.

Prayer (seeking the time to be still and quiet in the presence of Jesus):

Loving Lord Jesus,
thank you that you want to spend time with me (us).
Help me (us) to make the time to put aside the busyness of the day to be still and quiet in your presence.

CREATING 'CHURCH' AT HOME

Help me to be a good listener (us to be good listeners) to what you have to say to me (us), and to respond positively.
Help me (us) to allow myself (ourselves) to rest in your presence, and to be spiritually refreshed – especially when I am feeling anxious or my mood is low.
Also, encourage other people to rest in your presence and experience that same kind of refreshment.
Amen.

Finish with the Lord's Prayer.

Zacchaeus

Be still and quiet: Loved, accepted and transformed – all through meeting with Jesus.

Passage to read: Psalm 138.

(Option 1)
Resting in his presence: Meditate for a few moments on the fact that you are loved and accepted by Jesus – just as you are.

(Option 2)
Coffee time: Chat over a hot drink about the different areas of our lives that can benefit from the transforming power of the Holy Spirit. How would it feel to allow the Holy Spirit to work freely in your life?

(Option 3)
Make a plan (begin with the prayer – Lord, reveal your plan. Amen)**:** Which is the most important to you at this time: to be loved, accepted, valued, encouraged or respected by others? Do you think you might need to learn to love, accept, value, encourage and respect yourself?

Story to tell (in the author's words):
(Based on Luke 19:1-10)

> Zacchaeus was a chief tax collector, and he was wealthy. That, together with the fact that he worked for the Romans and was probably ripping off his

fellow countrymen, made him rather unpopular. As for his riches – material wealth has the habit of only satisfying for a limited time. The proof of the pudding was quite simply that, all in all, Zacchaeus was quite a sad person. Indeed, he really appeared to be searching for some kind of meaning and purpose to his life. And, I guess, for someone to love and accept him. It was in the course of this search that Zacchaeus wanted to see Jesus when he passed through Jericho. He had no aspirations to meet him – to see him would be sufficient.

Zacchaeus was far from tall, and no one was going to do him any favours like making room for him at the front of the crowd. He decided to climb a tree, so that he could see above people's heads.

The excitement and related level of noise increased considerably as Jesus was spotted in the distance.

'Get ready, he's on his way!'

Zacchaeus leaned forwards very carefully, for fear of losing his balance. He was reluctant to cheer too loudly, just in case he drew attention to himself. So he contented himself by having a fidget around to make himself comfortable, in preparation for the important moment. Remember that Zacchaeus just wanted to see Jesus – nothing more.

Zacchaeus could hardly contain his excitement as Jesus came ever closer. His gaze moved away from the large crowd below his perch – the same crowd to which he desired to be inconspicuous – and centred solely on Jesus. I repeat that Zacchaeus had no expectation for anything more than just to see Jesus.

Moments later, Jesus stopped under the tree – the same tree that Zacchaeus was sitting in. He looked up. 'Zacchaeus, come down. I was hoping to come to your house for some refreshments and a chat.'

Words probably failed Zacchaeus. He had only ever thought he would see Jesus, but now he was to meet him personally. This could change his whole life. There were murmurs among the crowd.

'Fancy taking notice of someone like him!'

'Who'd have thought Jesus would choose to be the guest of a sinner?!'

'It's not fair!'

But Zacchaeus already felt loved and accepted by Jesus.

The crowd waited in anticipation: Would this be 'payback' time for this sinner who had swindled them time and time again? They didn't have to wait too long to find out. It was a transformed Zacchaeus who hurried out with Jesus, carrying a large bag of money.

'I'm going to pay back all those people I have cheated – fourfold. And I am going to give half my money to the poor.'

The crowd were taken aback – speechless!

Jesus looked on with satisfaction: after all, his mission was – and still is – to seek and to save the lost.

The power of love and acceptance

Meeting with Jesus and entering into a personal relationship with him is life changing, with a significance that goes on forever – even after death. It's not just about feeling loved and accepted by him. Through that relationship, we are forgiven for all the things we have done wrong, and we are transformed by the indwelling Holy Spirit. And the evidence of such a relationship will be there for others to see and experience.

Living with anxiety or depression, it is easy to feel that society no longer accepts us in the same way – but Jesus loves and accepts us just as we are!

Prayer (giving thanks that we are loved and accepted by Jesus):

Lord Jesus,
thank you that you love and accept me (us) just as I am (we are).
Thank you that through meeting with you and entering into a personal relationship with you, I am (we are) forgiven and transformed – and my life is (our lives are) made complete.
Thank you that your mission is to seek and to save the lost.
Help me (us) to strive for an ever closer relationship with you, and to experience the transforming power of the Holy Spirit fully in my life (our lives).
Let the evidence of my (our) relationship with you be unmistakably present in my life (our lives) for others to experience.
I (We) pray for all those who are still seeking, in the same way that Zacchaeus is at the beginning of his story.
In your name.
Amen.

Finish with the Lord's Prayer.

Nicodemus

Be still and quiet: Physical death – and eternal life.

Passage to read: Psalm 39 (note in particular verse 7b).

(Option 1)
Resting in his presence: As you rest in God's presence, be assured in the knowledge that the eternal life Jesus speaks about in the Bible refers to being in God's presence forever.

(Option 2)
Coffee time: Chat over a hot drink about what you understand by the term 'eternal life'. Is that a comforting thought?

(Option 3)
Make a plan (begin with the prayer – Lord, reveal your plan. Amen): Choose some different coloured felt tip pens, coloured pencils, pastels or paints; and on a sheet of paper sketch or paint a picture of what you believe heaven will be like. Consider if this reflects in any way your interpretation of life here and now. Does that affect the plan?

Story to tell (in the author's words):
(Based on John 3:1-21)

> Why might someone deliberately decide to go out visiting at night when it's dark? Perhaps because they don't want to be seen by anyone!

Nicodemus was a Pharisee and a member of the Jewish ruling council. You could say that he was quite an important and influential person – and he did not want to be seen mixing with the likes of Jesus and his disciples for fear of repercussions. So he went to visit Jesus at night, to ask him some questions about things that had been puzzling him.

'To perform the amazing miracles that I've observed, you must be from God,' he began.

Jesus sensed that Nicodemus was curious about the kingdom of God and wanted to clarify the situation. 'There is only one way to enter into the kingdom, and that is by being born again.'

Nicodemus looked confused. 'How can someone be born a second time? It is not possible to enter into a mother's womb again.'

Jesus repeated, 'There is only one way to enter into the kingdom, and that is by being born again.' He clarified: 'Of the Spirit.'

Nicodemus still didn't understand. 'How can this happen?'

Jesus went on to predict his death on the cross, and to explain that as a result people would enter into God's eternal kingdom through believing in him. He emphasised how much God loved the world in order to do that: so that people could be saved from the consequences of sin.

Interestingly, later on Nicodemus accompanied Joseph of Arimathea to bury Jesus' body in the tomb – after his crucifixion. It would certainly appear that he had made a positive response to Jesus and his teaching.

Entering into a new life that is eternal

In a world where physical death is expected – and feared by many – Jesus offers the opportunity to enter into his eternal kingdom, and to live forever in his presence. The way into that kingdom is to place our belief in Jesus, to symbolically die to our old sinful lifestyle and to be reborn into a new lifestyle, living according to Jesus' teaching and example. We cannot be reborn in a physical sense, but we can be reborn spiritually! And it is possible to be reborn at any age!

Prayer (recognising and responding to the opportunity to be reborn into a new way of life):

Our loving heavenly Father,
thank you that you love me (us) so much that you allowed Jesus to die on the cross, paying the penalty for my (our) sin – and he rose again.
Thank you that as a result I (we) can be reborn spiritually and enter into the kingdom for ever.
Help me (us) to place my (our) belief in Jesus, to symbolically die to my (our) old sinful way(s) of life and to be reborn into a new way of life based on following Jesus' teaching and example.
Enable those who are searching to understand what it means to be reborn spiritually – and that it can happen at any age.
In Jesus' name.
Amen.

Finish with the Lord's Prayer.

The woman at the well

Be still and quiet: Hope.

Passage to read: Psalm 25.

(Option 1)
Resting in his presence: Spend some time quietly considering where your hope lies: is it primarily based on things like material wealth, or is it in the things of God?

(Option 2)
Coffee time: Chat over a hot drink about the transience of many of the things that people hold dear. Give some examples of such things. But without our health (mental or physical) what we hold valuable can change. What do you think?

(Option 3)
Make a plan (begin with the prayer – Lord, reveal your plan. Amen): Have you any hopes and dreams to add to the plan? When you have time, go through your notebook or computer file and summarise what you have written down under 'Make a plan'. You might like to formalise it: dividing it into different areas of your life, for example, family, friends, work, leisure, financial and faith. Include some achievable goals, encouragements, and hopes and dreams; and make a note of positive things you have learned as a result of your journey through anxiety and depression.

Story to tell (in the author's words):
(Based on John 4:1-26, 39-42)

Jesus arrived at Jacob's well in Samaria. He was hot and tired, so he found somewhere comfortable to sit. Soon a woman from that area approached to draw some water.

'Would you give a drink to a weary traveller?' Jesus asked.

The woman was aware that Jews and Samaritans didn't usually associate with each other, and asked, 'Are you sure you want me to get you a drink?'

'If you knew who I am,' Jesus replied, 'you would be asking me for the gift of living water.'

The woman was confused and argued, 'But you don't have a bucket to draw water from the well. Where are you going to get this living water from? Are you more powerful than Jacob who provided this well?'

Jesus smiled. 'If you drink of this living water, you will never be thirsty again. In fact, it will bring you eternal life.'

The woman said, 'All right, then; let me have some. Then I will never have to come to collect water from this well again.'

Jesus encouraged the woman, 'Go and fetch your husband to share in this conversation.'

'I don't have a husband,' came the reply.

'You have answered truthfully,' Jesus told her. 'The man you are living with is not your husband, though you have had five husbands in the past.'

The woman was amazed. 'You must be some kind of prophet to know that!' Then, trying to change the subject, she commented, 'There has been some dispute about where is the right place to worship.'

Jesus explained, 'The place of worship is not the real issue. The real issue is how you worship – remember salvation is coming through Jewish lines.'

'I've heard about the Messiah coming,' the woman replied.

There was a moment of silence before Jesus stated, 'I am the Messiah.'

Through the woman telling her friends and neighbours about meeting with Jesus, many Samaritans came to him and begged him to stay. As a result of Jesus staying on for another two days, and through his ministry, many believed that he really was the Saviour of the world, and they put their trust in him.

Discovering hope

This is a story primarily about being able to possess eternal hope. Jesus is still the one who offers salvation to us today. If we believe that he is the Messiah – the one who came to set humankind free from the consequences of sin – and we accept him as our Lord and Saviour, then we will receive that hope which nothing can take away. Maybe there are times, when living with anxiety or depression, we may feel that almost all we have left is that hope.

Prayer (giving thanks for and claiming the hope that is available through Jesus):

My (Our) Lord and Saviour Jesus Christ,
thank you that you are the one who came to earth to bring salvation to humankind.

Thank you that you have brought hope to a world that would otherwise be hopeless.

Help me (us) to believe and trust in you.

Forgive me (us) for the things I (we) have done wrong in my life (our lives), and help me (us) to accept you as my (our) Lord and Saviour.

Fill me (us) with eternal hope, particularly as I (we) face living with anxiety or depression, and sometimes everything becomes a struggle.

I (We) pray that you will lead all those who are feeling hopeless to discover hope through a relationship with you.

In your name.

Amen.

Finish with the Lord's Prayer.

PART FOUR

Additional resources

Prayers in response to how I'm feeling

Feeling frightened (I'm not sure what is happening)

Almighty God,

thank you that you are a powerful God and the God of miracles.

Right now, I need to feel your strong arms around me:
protecting me in this time of fear;
guiding me when everything seems uncertain;
holding me up, when I feel that my world is dropping away from underneath me;
being strong in my weakness.

I am fearful of what is happening as I feel anxious, my mood is low, I struggle to find the motivation to do every-day tasks, I am not sleeping well and my confidence has plummeted.

I am fearful of what the future holds, whether I will be able to cope and keep my independence.

Please be with me at all times:
surround me with your love;
grant me peace;
and fill me with eternal hope through my relationship with Jesus.

In his name.

Amen.

Feeling frightened (having been diagnosed with anxiety or depression)

Loving heavenly Father,
thank you that you are a powerful God.
    I need to experience your power in my life right now.
    I need to be able to overcome the fears.
    I need the strength and courage to move forwards in my life.
    I need the encouragement to carry on living life to the full.
I am feeling so fearful because I have been diagnosed with
anxiety (depression):
    fearful of what I know about the condition;
    fearful of what I don't know about how it will affect me;
    fearful of each new day;
    and too fearful to make any plans for the future.
Please stay with me during the good times and the difficult
ones, and never stop loving or caring for me.
And uphold my family and friends during the time ahead.
In Jesus' name.
Amen.

Feeling frightened (not being able to cope)

Gracious God,
thank you that you understand how I feel, and why I feel like
it – and that you care.
    It's one of my greatest fears.
    I don't feel that I am coping any more.
    Chores around my home and garden are being neglected.
Please help me to discover the motivation to carry out some
of the more basic tasks.
Help me to put aside some of the more difficult tasks that can
wait until I feel stronger and more confident.

Place around me people who are willing to take over those important tasks that can't wait and I really can't do myself. And take away the worry of those tasks that aren't going to get done at all.
In Jesus' name.
Amen.

Feeling frightened (no motivation and everything looks bleak)

Lord Jesus,
I need assurance concerning my immediate and eternal future:
to know that death is not the end;
to be reassured of my salvation through you;
to overcome the fear of dying – and the fears of living.
Thank you for your words in John 14, which say that:
your followers don't need to be worried or anxious – now or in the future;
you are preparing a place for us;
and you will come to take us to be with you there;
but in the meantime you are here with us, through the indwelling Holy Spirit.
Please help me to believe the promises in the Bible, and to find comfort and hope through them – now and for eternity – and in my relationship with you.
Amen.

Feeling lonely

Loving heavenly Father,
thank you that you are always with me. It is a great comfort, but I still feel lonely.
Loneliness isn't about me not realising that you are with me;

it's not even just about whether or not friends, family or others who care are in my home.

Loneliness can sometimes be about not being able to get out.

It can be about not feeling confident enough to get involved in activities.

It can be about feeling very self-conscious about living with anxiety or depression.

It can be about feeling that most of my friends and family don't understand.

It can be about isolation.

Please take away the loneliness I am feeling.

Help me to feel your presence in a very real way.

Lead members of the church family to visit me when I am at my lowest.

And enable me to find comfort in the words of Scripture.

In Jesus' name.

Amen.

Feeling confused, frustrated and emotional

Lord Jesus,

thank you that you understand the feelings I am going through at the present time – as a result of anxiety or depression.

The loneliness . . .

The tearfulness . . .

The loss of motivation . . .

The pointlessness . . .

The frustration . . .

The apprehension about the future . . .

The pain . . .

The wondering how to cope.

I need a comforting hug, and the reassurance that I will get through this.

Please place people around me who care:
  to offer comfort;
  friends who take the trouble to phone or visit;
  those who can offer some practical help;
  and someone who really means it when they say, 'Call me
  any time if you need something.'
Help me in my struggle with confusion, frustration and
heightened emotions.
Let there be more good days than bad.
Let the knowledge of my faith in you bring hope for the future.
Amen.

Feeling angry (Why me?)

Gracious heavenly Father,
thank you that you are a good listener.
I am feeling angry right now.
  It seems so unfair *(talk to God about your situation)*.
  I feel so irritated by people who make comments like,
  'That's life . . .'
  I keep asking the question, 'Why me?'
  I really, really struggle to ask the question, 'Why not me?'
I need the freedom to give that anger a voice to express itself
in a harmless way.
Please help me to accept my situation; and take away this
anger and feeling of injustice.
Grant me a generous and compassionate heart when people
make thoughtless or unhelpful comments.
In Jesus' name.
Amen.

Feeling hopeless

Eternal God,

living with anxiety or depression, I have feelings of hopelessness:

I used to love a new project to get my teeth into.

Holidays were something to look forward to.

I had such plans and ambitions.

Tomorrow was always another day, filled with new opportunities – a day to be looked forward to.

Now every day seems to be a struggle:

I find it so difficult to make plans.

I struggle to feel optimistic.

Thank you for the privilege of serving.

Please grant me purpose in my life still: a worthwhile task to perform.

Help me to feel needed by those around me.

Help me to set achievable goals – and to achieve them!

Fill me with hope: not just for eternity, but also for now.

In Jesus' name.

Amen.

CREATING
'CHURCH'
AT HOME

CREATING 'CHURCH' AT HOME SERIES

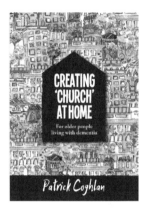

For older people
living with dementia
1501517

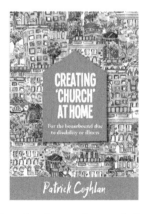

For the housebound due
to disability or illness
1501519

For the elderly
housebound
1501520

Find more books by Patrick
at www.kevinmayhew.com